One-to-One Training and Coaching Skills

One-to-One Training and Coaching Skills

ROGER BUCKLEY   JIM CAPLE

San Diego • Toronto • Amsterdam • Sydney

First published in 1991 by Kogan Page, in association with the Institute of Training and Development.

Kogan Page Limited
120 Pentonville Road
London N1 9JN

Published in the United States of America by
Pfeiffer & Company
8517 Production Avenue
San Diego, CA 92121-2280
(619) 578-5900
FAX (619) 578-2042

British Library Cataloguing in Publication Data

A CIP record for this book is available from the British Library.

ISBN 0 7494 0394 2

Contents

Series Editor's Foreword

Organizations get things done when people do their jobs effectively. To make this happen they need to be well trained. A number of people are likely to be involved in this training: identifying the needs of the organization and of the individual, selecting or designing appropriate training to meet those needs, delivering it and assessing how effective it was. It is not only 'professional' or full-time trainers who are involved in this process; personnel managers, line managers, supervisors and job holders are all likely to have a part to play.

This series has been written for all those who get involved with training in some way or another, whether they are senior personnel managers trying to link the goals of the organization with training needs or job holders who have been given responsibility for training newcomers. Therefore, the series is essentially a practical one which focuses on specific aspects of the training function. This is not to say that the theoretical underpinnings of the practical aspects of training are unimportant. Anyone seriously interested in training is strongly encouraged to look beyond 'what to do' and 'how to do it' and to delve into the areas of why things are done in a particular way.

The authors have been selected because they have considerable practical experience. All have shared, at some time, the same difficulties, frustrations and satisfactions of being involved in training and are now in a position to share with others some helpful and practical guidelines.

In this book, Jim Caple and I consider one-to-one training and coaching which, unfortunately, have come to be known as 'Sitting by Nellie'. In many organizations it would appear that there is a belief that simply by sitting and observing, learning will occur by some form of

7

psychological osmosis. Some recognition of the demanding nature of training individuals has been shown by those who rightly claim that the success of such training depends on how good Nellie is. However, the answer to the question 'good at what?' usually points towards technical proficiency rather than competence and skill as a trainer. In order to be effective, trainers not only need to be technically proficient but they need to be able to plan, prepare and deliver structured sessions which take account of using the most appropriate learning strategies and tactics to train and develop individuals.

ROGER BUCKLEY

1 How Training Fits into the Organization

▷   SUMMARY   ◁

In this chapter you will learn about:
- The value of proper training to organizations and to individuals.
- The nature of investment needed for effective training.
- A systematic approach to training.
- A model for one-to-one training.

Training has always played an important part in many kinds of human learning. The survival of the race has been an instinctive motivator to learn and to teach since the advent of the earliest form of mankind. Throughout the ages, craftsmen have passed on their skills to their apprentices and as new skills and techniques have been developed, they too have been taught to younger generations. As individuals, we have been trained from birth to feed ourselves, to take care of our bodies, to learn how to play and to socialize, and to develop those skills needed to begin a formal education and subsequently enter the world of work.

Most of us would see this process as normal and logical and we would expect such a process to continue throughout our working and social lives. However, the fact that training can make an important, if not crucial, contribution to the health, development and effectiveness of an organization often seems to have been overlooked. In order to survive and to prosper all organizations have to adapt in a flexible way to political, economic, social and technological changes. The success they achieve in managing such adaptations will be decided partly by how well they use and develop the people who work for them. In recent years there has been a greater appreciation of the important part played by all forms of training in this process.

Unfortunately, even some of the well-intentioned organizations and their enthusiastic trainers cannot be successful if their efforts are misdirected because they do not know some of the basic functions and purpose of sound training and because they are not aware of the common pitfalls.

Misdirected effort can come about for a number of reasons:

- An organization may run some of its training programmes because it has always done so. The training may have become almost part of the organization's tradition and nobody has questioned the reasons for such programmes or their value. They often remain unchanged in content and design despite changes in the jobs which have been brought about by new technology, methods, structures and processes.
- Departments and sections within the organization may wish to 'use up' money in their budgets before the end of the financial year and before the money is 'clawed' back. Training may be seen as a valid excuse for such expenditure as it may project the right image of a department or section to the rest of the organization or to higher management.
- For whatever reason an employee may have some spare time available in his or her work schedule and training is often regarded as a sensible way of 'taking up the slack'. The justification, often put forward for employing a valuable time resource in this manner, is that training will contribute to an individual's development although development for what is usually left rather vague or to the imagination.
- The 'flavour of the year' syndrome is familiar in the training world. Organizations run or send people on courses using the latest training approach to a particular perennial theme, being swept along by the initial enthusiasm for the approach, without analysing in any real depth its relevance to their particular needs.

What Training is

Training should be a systematically planned investment in the development of the knowledge, skills and attitudes needed by an individual to perform a job to a satisfactory level. It is a partnership between trainee and trainer who work together to achieve the learning levels needed to meet the demands of the job. This means that once a basic level of proficiency has been achieved, the former trainee continues to develop in speed and accuracy until reaching the level of an experienced worker. This process of training and development should be continuous as trainees progress from one job to another in the organization.

The most obvious and more valid reasons which support this idea of continuous training and development are that:

- No job can be performed without adequate training.
- Improvements in job performance can only be brought about by a programme of relevant instruction.
- The only way of correcting inadequate or incorrect job performance is by remedial training.
- Line and staff managers have a responsibility for managing their money, manpower and material resources effectively and training, as a practical day-to-day activity, is part of this management problem.

Training can take various forms and these include courses, one-to-one training, coaching, computer-based training, learning packages, videos, job guides, etc.

The forms of training on which this book concentrates are those which are conducted on a one-to-one basis. The descriptions of the following terms help to clarify what is being discussed.

On-the-job training, which may include one-to-one instruction or coaching, is training that takes place in the normal workplace of the trainee and covers the knowledge, skills and attitudes appropriate to the correct performance of a task or job. It may represent the whole of a training programme or it may be part of a programme which includes off-the-job training.

Off-the-job training is training which takes place away from the job location. Usually, this form of training takes the form of courses which are provided either by the organization's own training department or by an 'outside' training organization. Other forms of off-the-job training include the use of personal learning packages, computer-based training etc.

One-to-one instruction is helping a trainee to acquire knowledge and skills so that he or she can perform a particular task or job.

Coaching is developing the ability and experience of trainees by giving them systematically planned and progressively more 'stretching' tasks to perform, coupled with continuous appraisal and counselling.

On-the-job instruction is normally used when the trainee is naïve and new to the task or job in question. Coaching, on the other hand, is about helping a trainee to extend, improve or develop already acquired basic skills.

Supporting is not actually training. The role is more pastoral by nature. The function of the supporter is to support those working on personal learning programmes by discussing problems and progress, giving encouragement, acting as a sounding board and generally looking after the interests of individuals who have no direct contact with tutors or other students.

What Training is not

Before concentrating on the value and purpose of training as a whole, it is worthwhile to examine specifically some common approaches to one-to-one training which are far from being effective. A popular description of one-to-one training is 'Sitting by Nellie'. The assumption here is that by sitting alongside someone performing the job, the trainee will pick up the necessary knowledge, skills and procedures to do the job themselves or that they will be shown how to do it. Job holders are often asked 'to show' newcomers how the job is done. This makes their training, at best, a hit-or-miss affair because assumptions have to be made that the job holder is both competent at the job and sufficiently interested and skilled in one-to-one training techniques to be able to undertake the training. Even when this assumption has been met, the job holder is often faced by the constraints of not being able to organize the training in the most appropriate sequence nor being able to spend sufficient time on it. This is because they have to continue to do the job and undertake the training at the same time. Situations such as this all too often place the onus of responsibility for learning on the trainee.

A number of line managers and supervisors have been heard to say that they go in for or believe in 'deep end training'. In fact, this is a contradiction in terms. Many people have experienced being 'thrown in at the deep end' but this treatment cannot be made legitimate by putting the word 'training' behind it; it is, more accurately, an excuse not to train. While it is possible for people to find out for themselves through some form of discovery learning, deficiencies in their performance may not be noticed for some time. Safety procedures could be ignored, important stages in procedures and processes omitted and unauthorized decisions could be made. Unfortunately, the blame for poor performance is placed on the individual who has not been trained properly rather than on the line managers who should have been responsible for that training. This becomes even more acute when the untrained workers, with their 'bad habits', are subsequently given the responsibility for training others.

The Value of Training

Benefits to the Organization

Systematically planned training results in benefits to the organization and to those individuals who have been involved in the training programme. In general terms, the greatest value of training is that it helps the organization to achieve its objectives. Clearly defined objectives should stem from the organization's goals and then should be passed or 'cascaded' down the organization to form the basis of departmental and unit objectives and, finally, to provide objectives for individual workers. It can be seen then that corporate or organizational goals are achieved by people doing their jobs properly, and to do this they need to be trained. In some cases corporate objectives are related to profits, whereas in non-profit-making organizations, targets are related to speed and efficiency of service within a given budget.

Having a well-trained staff also means that productivity and quality are likely to be higher because employees are able to work faster and more accurately. This, in turn, results in less wastage of materials or time. A high-quality product or a first-class service is likely to reduce complaints from customers or, more positively, to raise the level of prestige of the organization. Another way of looking at the benefits to the organization is to consider the ways in which it can make use of a trained workforce. When staff are used to participating in training programmes, their level of trainability increases. This means that they are more easily and more quickly trained on new or additional tasks which gives a greater level of flexibility in the use of the workforce at all levels.

Benefits for the Individual

It is not solely the organization that benefits from good training. Those individuals who participate in training activities are likely to find that they benefit personally. Everyone likes to feel that they are competent at their job and training helps to give them greater personal satisfaction from the experience of being able to perform a job well and from being able to exercise new skills, techniques and procedures. This is particularly the case when customers or clients recognize and appreciate that expertise. This, in turn, leads to an increased level of confidence which often results in a raising of morale and team spirit as people realize that they are making a valued contribution to the work of the organization.

Naturally, material benefits are equally important and increased earnings and opportunities for promotion which come through improved performance are further benefits which might follow.

Benefits of Training to the Organization and to the Individual

There are some benefits of training that can be shared by both the organization and by the people who staff it. This is probably best described as the occupational health of the organization. Staff who are well-trained are able to meet the challenges of the job, cope with difficulties and enjoy a high level of job satisfaction. In short, there is a high level of morale. When this is the case, there is likely to be a lower turnover rate of staff and less absenteeism. One of the reasons given most frequently by leavers, especially those who have been recruited directly from school, is lack of training. If staff do not enjoy their work because they are not equipped to perform efficiently then the slightest reason for staying away on medical grounds will be found and in some cases no reason is needed at all.

It is recognized that other factors contribute to performance and job satisfaction. Bad management and inadequate supervision are high on the list of reasons given by leavers. However, training is again at the root of this and points to the fact that training should be continuous and should be directed at all levels of the organization. For example, supervisors are often selected on the basis of their technical expertise without any thought being given to training them as supervisors. The result of this could be dissatisfaction all round.

When morale is high it is easier to foster a corporate spirit and when pro-active training is a regular and an integral part of organizational life, it is easier for changes to corporate objectives, organizational structure or any form of innovation to be introduced without threat and possibly even to be welcomed with enthusiasm.

The benefits of training felt and shared by both the organization and trainees can often develop enthusiasm towards the process of learning and development. This may, in turn, help to create a 'learning organization' that is more flexible in dealing with and responding to present and future demands.

Investment in Training

While many organizations have shown their commitment to off-the-job training, it is disappointing to find that the importance and significance of on-the-job training often seems to be ignored or underestimated. Sloman (1989) suggests that '... the legion of people who deliver on-the-job training in the office, on the factory floor and at the construction site are neither recognized nor recorded – and in almost all cases are not trained to train'. A research survey carried out on behalf of the Training Commission (UK) and reported by Sloman (1989), provided some very interesting findings (Figure 1.1).

VOLUMES AND COSTS OF TRAINING

In 1986–7 employers in Great Britain provided 125.4 million days of training in total:

    64 7 million days off-the-job
    60.7 million days on-the-job

On average, each employee received 7 days training a year:

    3.6 days off-the-job
    3.4 days on-the-job

But more than half the employees received no training at all.

In 1986–7 employers in Great Britain spent £14.4 billion in total on the provision of training for their workforce – just over £800 per employee:

    £5.8 billion on off-the-job training
    £6.8 billion on on-the-job training
    £1.8 billion on training overheads.

Figure 1.1 *Key findings from the Training Commission survey on employers' training activities*

These figures indicate that training delivered on-the-job accounted for at least half of the total training undertaken. In addition, it would seem that a great deal of on-the-job training is of the one-to-one variety and that between one and two million people in the United Kingdom act as on-the-job trainers. No doubt these would include line managers and supervisors, job holders 'handing over' their duties to new incumbents and specifically-designated staff trainers who come 'on site' to instruct. Bearing all this in mind, one of the key conclusions to be drawn from the Training Commission survey should come as no surprise:

> A major effort to improve the quality of on-the-job training would pay considerable benefits to most employers.

These potential benefits come about particularly because of the advantages of on-the-job training over off-the-job training and these are:

Time. It is likely to take less time to train somebody at or near their job location than to send them on a training course. Training courses often cover both the 'need to know' and the 'nice to know' features whereas on-the-job training can be tailored specifically to meet the essential needs of a particular trainee.

Flexibility. On-the-job training can be flexibly 'fitted around' the individual concerned and the circumstances in which he or she works.

Cost. The overall costs of on-the-job training can be less than off-the-job training for two main reasons. Firstly, there may be less interference with production and secondly, if the subject expert is available and has been adequately trained as a one-to-one trainer, then such training will be more effective.

Transfer. It may be easier to transfer what has been learned in what is close to real job conditions than from simulated conditions employed on a training course. The delay before being fully operational caused by having to make adjustments when trying to apply on-the-course skills, etc. to real job conditions can be another reason for off-the-job training costs being higher than on-the-job training.

Why, given these advantages, has less attention been paid to on-the-job training and in particular to one-to-one instruction and coaching? There have been two fundamental and interrelated assumptions which, unfortunately, have meant that in many circumstances these types of training have been introduced and conducted in a less than professional manner. The first of these assumptions is that one-to-one training is a natural and familiar process. This assumption has its origins in the earliest form of training and learning given by parent to child. There are also historical precedents to be found in craft apprenticeships. Many master craftsmen were highly motivated trainers, as they were an integral part of the process of ensuring continuity within their craft. Similarly, these kinds of relationship are found between personal tutors and pupils in private and higher institutes of learning. However, despite our familiarity with some of these forms of learning and teaching, it is neither logically nor factually correct to conclude that being an effective one-to-one trainer or coach will come naturally to everyone.

The second assumption is that having expertise or skill in a subject or discipline is linked with the ability to teach or educate others in that field. The attitudes engendered by the traditions of the well-rounded and motivated amateur remain very strong in training where it is often believed that if the technical expertise is available within a particular area, any associated training problem will be solved automatically.

From this, it can be seen that there are a number of precedents and prejudices to persuade people into accepting the view that the ability to be an effective one-to-one instructor or coach is a natural and widely dispersed phenomenon. It seems that training or coaching by 'Sitting by Nellie' is regarded by many as simply a matter of observing an expert, and learning occurring by some process of psychological osmosis. Furthermore, there is a tendency to be complacent about, or even antagonistic towards, the notion of, and the need for, the training of 'Nellies' and coaches.

With these attitudes prevailing, it is hardly surprising that the training of instructors and coaches is often a hit-or-miss affair leading to inconsistent results. Such unpredictable outcomes have, no doubt, helped these forms of training to acquire unprofessional connotations.

Given this situation, there is an obvious requirement for the basic assumptions about 'Nellie'-type training and coaching to be examined critically. In many circumstances it will be necessary to replace 'Sitting by Nellie' with systematically designed training and properly trained one-to-one trainers and coaches.

None of the benefits of training can be had for nothing. Bland statements about commitment to training are not enough; commitment has to be backed by investment at corporate level and at every unit and sub-unit level in the organization. Investment from the top of the organization is usually in the form of money and facilities but these resources cannot be used if line managers, particularly in the lower echelons, find that they cannot spare sufficient time or experienced staff to run a training programme. This is when they have to resort to 'deep end' or 'Nellie' tactics. This means that the investment must include staffing to a level which allows training to take place without operational functions being jeopardized. In addition, managers at all levels need to be familiarized with the function and process of training. This includes an appreciation of the amount of preparation time that trainers need and the skills that they have to employ, as well as an understanding of how people learn.

At unit and at sub-unit level the real and practical investment in time is more clearly felt because of the likely interruptions to operational functions. However, sub-unit managers and supervisors must support trainers in their efforts to plan systematically and to deliver effective training and coaching.

A Systematic Approach to Training

There is nothing complex about a systematic approach to training. Most disciplines or activities are approached systematically; for example, we would not begin to hang new wallpaper without first stripping the old paper from the walls and making good any damage. The same basic principle of doing things in the right order applies to any systematic approach which it might be more appropriate to describe as a logical or common sense approach.

In training, this systematic approach is usually presented diagramatically as a working tool or job guide for trainers and as such is liable to some variance. However, there are four key activities which are essential in the process. They are: finding out who needs training and in what, designing and planning the training, conducting the training, and then finding out how effective the training was (Figure 1.2).

The training needs represent the mismatch between what the job demands and what the prospective trainee possesses in knowledge, skills, attitudes and experience. This stage of identifying the needs is clearly important so that the trainees do not become the victims of too much or too little training. It separates the 'need to know' from the 'nice to know'. Too little training will leave them inadequate to the demands of the job, demotivated and in need of further training. Too much training can result in expectations on the part of the trainee that cannot be met and which leads to low morale. In both cases unnecessary expense is incurred.

Designing and planning the training is not a task to be undertaken in a hurry. A considerable amount of time needs to be invested in working out the training content, the sequence in which it can best be presented, the most appropriate learning strategies to use, the equipment and other resources that are needed to support the training and the amount of time that it will take. Trainers at all levels must be given time to plan and prepare if they are expected to do a thorough job.

The delivery stage most trainers are familiar with. In some organizations the identification of needs and the design of training have been undertaken by someone else in the training department. When this is the case, those delivering the training should ensure that they know what the precise training needs are and the rationale behind the design and structure of the training if they expect to train effectively. As has

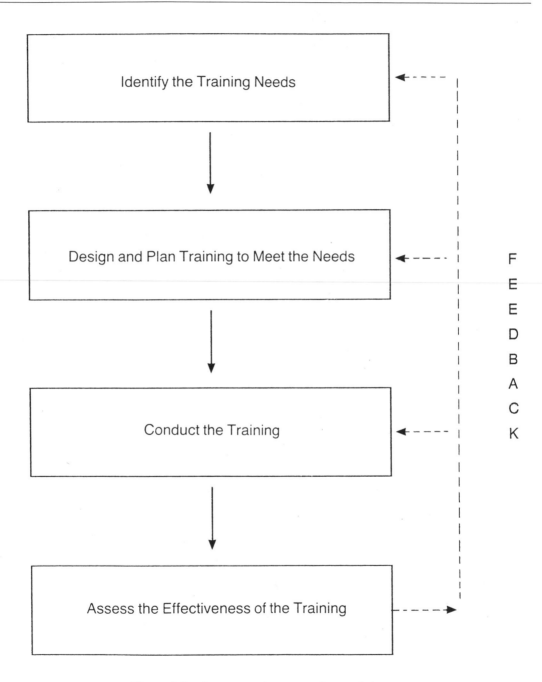

Figure 1.2 *A systematic approach to training*

been described earlier, delivering the training is not merely 'showing' or 'telling' but the application of a number of skills to assist the learning of the trainee. These skills will be covered in detail in Chapter 4.

There is little point in undertaking any training unless there is follow-up to see whether it has worked. This stage has been a weak link in many training programmes. If organizations have seen the value of investing in training, it follows that everyone involved should want to see if that investment was worthwhile. Often it is only those who have been trainees who know how well they have been trained and very little is fed back to the trainer. It is only by assessing the effectiveness of the training that use can be made of the feedback loop to remedy any deficiencies in the former trainee's performance, the structure of the training and the way in which it was delivered.

A Model for One-to-one Training

Having looked at a systematic approach to training, it can be appreciated that several models, frameworks or guidelines could be produced for each stage of the model. In particular, the delivery stage is one for which many different frameworks could be produced depending on the mode of delivery or which of the three main skill areas is being addressed. These main skills areas are:

Interpersonal skills eg, interviewing clients, telephone techniques, dealing face-to-face with customers, counselling staff, dealing with problems with people, etc.

Physical/practical skills eg, operating a lathe, repairing machinery or engines, sawing wood, wiring plugs, preparing vegetables, etc.

Procedural skills eg, filling in an application form for a bank loan, filling in an order form, costing an order, updating a mailing list, etc.

The model which is presented here as a guide to one-to-one training (Figure 1.3), is based on what is practised by good one-to-one trainers. It was developed by observing a number of trainers who had been reported by their managers as being particularly good. A model for coaching is described in Chapter 5.

The preparation stage is the foundation for successful training. Time invested at this stage pays a worthwhile dividend for the trainee,

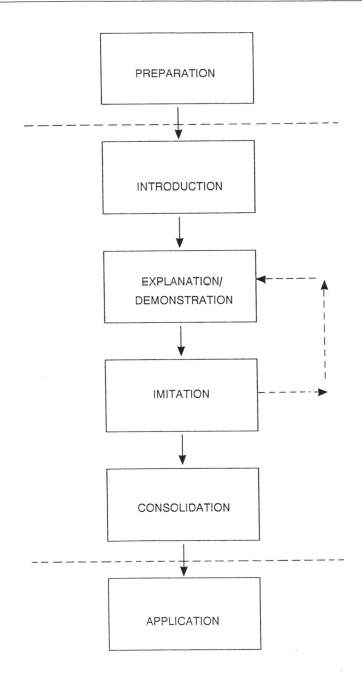

Figure 1.3   *A Model for One-to-One Training*

the trainer and the organization. The stages of introduction, explanation/demonstration, imitation and consolidation are stages during which the skills of one-to-one training are exercised by the trainer. The stage of application is the period after the completion of training when the former trainee puts into practice what he or she has learned. All too often the trainer loses interest or ceases to accept responsibility or accountability for the performance of trainees once they have completed their training. Each stage of the model will be discussed in detail in Chapter 1. However, earlier, attention was drawn to the importance of, and the need for, investment in time for preparation and this area needs to be considered first with particular emphasis being placed on the learner.

2 How and Why People Learn

▷   SUMMARY   ◁

In this chapter you will learn about:
- The physical and mental activities that assist learning.
- The motivation and readiness of trainees to participate in learning activities.
- Conditions and principles of learning.
- Individual differences.

In the last chapter it was shown that an organization's success comes from people being able to do their jobs properly. However, if they do not want to learn or they have difficulty in learning certain tasks, the trainer becomes somewhat impotent. It follows that it would be valuable for trainers to have an understanding of how and why people learn so that they can devise and prepare learning strategies that will help their trainees to become proficient more easily and to experience a greater level of personal satisfaction.

It could be felt that this is all too theoretical when what we are really interested in are the practicalities of getting people trained. However, the principles of how and why people learn are well within the experience of most of us, whether we are trainers or not. By reflecting on learning that we may have experienced in the past, many of the ideas discussed here will be found to be familiar.

Ways of Learning

Basically, people learn new knowledge and skills by means of five physical and mental activities. These are: trial and error, mental organization, behaviour modelling, use of language, and reflection.

1. Trial and Error

This activity is used when the learner tries to find the best way of doing something. Many of us have used this approach when trying to put together self-assembly furniture. When it is found that assembling parts in a particular sequence or using a particular technique leads to a satisfying and correct outcome, then we are likely to use that sequence and technique again. However, if that approach had resulted in damage, anger, parts in the wrong place, etc, it is most unlikely that we would approach it in that way again. Instead, by trial and error, other ways would be experimented with until a successful outcome was achieved.

In the catering industry trainee chefs use trial and error until they reach a consistency, flavour or appearance of food which is of the standard of perfection that they are looking for. In other jobs trainees may have to find the easiest or best way for them to hold and use particular instruments or tools, especially if they are left-handed and are being taught by a right-handed trainer. In learning some tasks the trainer may find it an advantage to allow the trainees to discover for themselves the best way for them as individuals to handle tools and materials.

2. Mental Organization

This method is when the learner attempts to put together a 'mental picture' of what has to be learned and then uses this mental map as a guide. For example, at certain stages of learning to drive a car, a learner driver may put together a mental image of the sequence of actions that have to be followed. These might include 'check mirror, indicate, pull out to overtake', etc. Once the trainee becomes familiar with the 'drill', these actions become automatic and the driver will not necessarily remain consciously aware of the mental picture or image that he or she had to use at the beginning.

3. Behaviour Modelling

This form of learning stems from our earliest years. Very young children are often seen observing intently the actions of their parents at work or other children at play and then trying to imitate them. They are trying to model themselves or their behaviour on what they have observed in others. This method of learning is used extensively in all forms of training. Sport provides numerous illustrations; for example, tennis coaches demonstrate to their pupils how a particular stroke should be played so that they can imitate the actions. Similarly, where the use of interpersonal skills has to be learned, the trainee may 'shadow' an experienced worker or the trainer to observe how different situations are dealt with so that they can approach them in a similar way. This might include giving advice to a customer, dealing with a complaint, handling a disciplinary problem, etc.

4. Use of Language

Perhaps it seems too obvious to include the fact that much learning takes place through the use of the written and the spoken word. However, it is worth emphasizing that because language is such a powerful medium we should ensure that it is used correctly and effectively. Trainers need to ensure that explanations are clear and concise and that they are not jargon-ridden. This is not to say that jargon should not be used – jargon has to be learned so that workers can communicate with one another. However, the key issue is that the jargon or technical language should be understood. Learning can be reinforced by the written word in the form of handouts, job guides, diagrams and notes written by the trainees themselves.

5. Reflection

This method of learning is similar to mental organization and, in many cases, follows on from learning by trial-and-error, behaviour modelling or the use of language. It is a process of thinking through or mulling over particular learning experiences in order to draw out lessons that can be applied in the future. For example, a trainee who is learning to interview, is observed by a trainer and given feedback on what went well and areas for improvement. The trainee is then able to reflect on his or her performance and on the feedback in order to improve or modify the way in which he or she conducts subsequent interviews.

These five forms of learning do not tend to function on their own, they work in combination. However, as will be seen later, certain ways of learning are more productive and more applicable in particular situations depending upon what has to be learned and upon the attitudes, abilities and past experiences of the learners.

Readiness of the Learner

The seeds of new learning are likely to fall on stony ground unless the trainee is 'ready'. The readiness of a trainee can be looked at from several standpoints – intellectual, motivational, emotional or physical. Although these will be discussed separately, in reality they are often interrelated and lead to either positive or negative results for the trainee or the trainer.

1. Intellectual Readiness

All trainees bring something with them to any new learning situation. This will include previous experience, a level of existing knowledge, specific skills, special aptitudes, general potential and capacity for learning etc. These skills and aptitudes might be mechanical, numerical, clerical, etc. This will have a bearing on how ready they are to undertake the training that is being planned for them. In some cases it may be necessary to introduce some basic or even remedial training before proper training can begin. In other cases it may be possible to speed up the training or even omit some of it if the trainees have already mastered some of the skills or have sufficient knowledge. For example a trainee who already has some experience of bookkeeping may not need to cover the basics in learning a new job in an accounts department.

2. Motivational Readiness

It is obvious, but nevertheless worth emphasizing, that learning is affected badly if the trainee has no desire or is not motivated, to learn. More positively, it is a rewarding experience for both the trainee and the trainer when the level of motivation to learn is high. There are a number of factors that potentially might influence trainees' motivation. These include meeting their needs, rewards and incentives and the perceptions, expectations and attitudes that they hold.

Meeting Needs
There are four categories of need which can be met by training:

Safety needs

These needs relate to the security that can be achieved through training. This is when the trainees know that they can undertake potentially dangerous tasks safely and without danger to themselves.

Emotional needs　　These needs are satisfied when trainees are able to see that learning new skills and acquiring additional knowledge will affect their job performance by giving them more control and independence in what they do and by giving them a feeling of achievement, self-confidence, autonomy, approval, acceptance and recognition in the eyes of other workers, and a feeling of belonging.

Intellectual needs　　Being able to master new skills and new knowledge is stimulating for many trainees. They need variety in what they do and the opportunity to exercise curiosity in finding out about the what, why and how of the learning that they are undertaking.

Self-fulfilment needs　　Most people like to feel that they have 'got somewhere' and in this respect training or learning helps to provide a meaning and sense of purpose.

Which of the above needs are important for any particular individual will depend on his or her personality, background and experience.

Rewards and incentives
Broadly speaking, there are two main forms of reward or incentive that are linked with learning. There are those rewards that are closely associated with the task itself which are called 'intrinsic' and those which are more in the way of being an outcome of performing the task, which are called 'extrinsic'.

Intrinsic rewards　　come from the sheer satisfaction that comes from being able to do the job properly. Preparing a neat column of figures that balance, receiving the thanks of a satisfied customer, building a good-looking house, etc, are all activities that provide intrinsic rewards.

Extrinsic rewards　　are quite independent of the task and include such rewards as money, promotion, enhanced career prospects etc. Therefore, the task itself could be boring and not intrinsically rewarding but the incentives that go with it provide the motivation. For example, the task of fitting two or three nuts and bolts to a component on an assembly line may be tedious but the worker is rewarded by a high pay packet. Similarly, someone may view the prospect of a spell in another department as boring but their motivation level is increased if they know that it is a step towards promotion.

The trainer is likely to have to arouse these intrinsic and extrinsic motivators in order to stimulate interest and effort in the trainee.

Perceptions, expectations and attitudes
Trainees are unlikely to make the effort to learn a new skill and

perform to the appropriate level unless they are convinced that the learning will lead to certain rewards in the short or long term. The trainer must ensure that the link between effort and reward is clearly established and eventually forged in the trainee's mind. Unfulfilled expectations will not only adversely affect the attitude of the person having undertaken the training but also the attitudes of other trainees as a result of informal communication such as the 'grapevine'.

Furthermore, the attitudes of trainees can be affected quite dramatically by the behaviour of the trainer. The trainer's skills and enthusiasm, or lack of it, will be a major influence on the trainees' achievements and their feelings towards the training experience.

3. Emotional Readiness

There is no doubt that the attitudes and enthusiasm of the trainer are important influences on how well the trainee learns a particular skill. However, trainers must guard against being over-exuberant and 'priming the motivational pump' too much. 'Hyping up' or stimulating high motivation before and during training may create anxiety and apprehension in some trainees. This is particularly the case if the trainer, at the same time, minimizes and is unrealistic about the difficulties of learning complex tasks. These emotions may be felt by the trainees because of doubts and fears aroused by the memory of previous failures in their earlier experiences of educational or occupational learning environments. The trainer's sensitivity, style and approach throughout the training or coaching process, but especially in the early stages, can go a long way to eliminate, or at least lessen, any emotional blockages and barriers that might interfere with subsequent learning. Specific techniques which trainers can employ are discussed in Chapter 4.

4. Physical Readiness

A trainee's physical readiness is as important, in some circumstances, as the aspects of readiness already discussed. This should be dealt with at the stage when the trainees are being selected for the one-to-one instruction or coaching programme. The potential employee specification should provide a guide to any essential physical requirements, eg, fitness, visual acuity, hearing, etc. that the trainee has to meet to be regarded as suitable to undertake the programme. For example, the layout of the cab of a crane may be such that height is an important factor. It could be that in some cases people with very short legs couldn't operate the foot controls properly. On the other hand, there may be cases where very tall people would be too cramped to work comfortably in the closed environment of the cab. In addition, there may be physical conditions, such as ill health, physical injury or fatigue that would require the trainer or coach to withdraw a trainee from a programme or session.

General Conditions Affecting Learning

The trainer must engage the trainee in the learning process in an active fashion. Before looking at some of the specific things that the trainee and the trainer have to do to make this happen, some attention must be paid to the general conditions within the learning situation that positively promote, or that are conducive to, learning.

Apart from stimulating the trainee's motivation, and not ignoring the importance of individual differences, the trainer must also 'arrange' the learning environment so as to maintain the trainee's alertness throughout. Trainers must be concerned with stimulating arousal and maintaining attention in the trainee during individual training or coaching sessions. A number of techniques can be used to present trainees with varied and novel stimulation. The trainer can employ visual aids, vary the pitch, pace and tone of voice, change his or her physical position or that of the trainee, introduce humour and, where feasible, vary the specific activity of the trainee. It is also helpful if trainees have the opportunity to talk with their trainer in order to seek assistance and to confirm progress, which will contribute to increasing their attention level. Furthermore, by continually demonstrating or illustrating the significance of what is being taught, through credible and relevant examples, the trainer should be able to maintain the trainees' interest. In addition, in order to combat mental or physical fatigue, the trainer should build into the training or coaching programme 'natural' breaks, rest periods and relaxtion slots. Trainers must also be keenly aware of the potential problem of overloading trainees with too much new material to learn, particularly those individuals of lower ability and those who have been out of training and education for some time.

Apart from taking account of the above considerations, the trainer must ensure that neither environment nor psychological conditions have a negative impact on the trainee's motivation and learning performance. It goes without saying that physical conditions such as poor lighting, inadequate ventilation and heating and uncomfortable seating can severely hamper or act as a major distraction or barrier to effective learning. The trainer must also create and maintain a supportive and understanding emotional climate.

A feature of the climate which the trainer should control is the degree of competition that is encouraged or comparisons of standards with other trainees. Although, in some circumstances, healthy competition can have beneficial effects on a trainee's performance or progress, it can also be counter-productive and have a detrimental effect on the trainee's current achievement and, probably more critically, on his or her attitude to subsequent training. It is better that a trainee competes against him or herself rather than waste energy competing against another real or fictional trainee.

Specific Conditions and Principles Affecting Learning

As well as being aware of the ways in which people learn and the general conditions that affect learning the trainer must also understand how specific conditions and principles of learning can be applied. In particular, the trainer must know how the organization of the material, the activities of the trainer and the involvement of the trainee will influence the way in which the aims of the training are achieved.

Sequencing the Training Material

Ensuring that the training content follows some logical order or an order that makes sense to the trainee, will make learning and subsequent recall and application much easier.

There are a number of 'laws' which help the trainer to arrange material in the best order:

— *Proceed from the easy or simple to the difficult or complex*
This seems a fairly commonsense principle to follow. In many tasks learners must acquire basic knowledge or skill before progressing to more complex material or situations. Moving on to the latter too quickly, before the fundamentals are in place, is often a recipe for failure.

— *Proceed from what the trainee knows to new or unknown material*
The trainer must try to build on what the trainee already knows or can already do. Forging a link between the known and the unknown will usually make new learning much easier, not least because learners may feel less anxious handling or dealing with material that they have some familiarity with. For example, a

bricklayer would feel more confident learning how to build an arch if he had already mastered the skills of building a straight wall. Similarly, customer-service officers would feel more confident in learning to deal directly with customers if they had first been given a good foundation in product knowledge and procedures.

— *Proceed from the practical or concrete to the more abstract and theoretical*

People will eventually learn general principles or rules if, initially, those principles or rules have been demonstrated or illustrated by way of concrete examples. Asking them to acquire abstract principles in 'isolation', without first clearly showing the principles being applied to specific and relevant situations, will hinder the build-up of their knowledge and understanding. For example, it would be better to show a trainee chef how to cook vegetables to the desired level of firmness or consistency before going on to explain how cooking affects the nutritional values of food.

Whole Versus Part Learning

Another important consideration is whether or not to cover what has to be learned as a whole or in parts. For instance, if the skill to be learned is made up of several elements, should they be learned all at once or should the trainee be taught the elements separately, before combining them into the whole? The answer to this question seems to be 'it depends'. The whole-method is more advantageous than the part-method when:

- the learner is intelligent (making a very able person learn a series of easy parts may have an adverse effect on motivation);
- the learning of, and practice on, the task or skill is spread out over time rather than massed into a short time frame;
- the task or skill is not particularly complex and the elements which make it up seem to 'fit' together naturally.

Setting Objectives and Sub-objectives

In order to stimulate and sustain a trainee's motivation, the trainer can outline, at the beginning of the programme, the learning objective to be achieved or show the trainee what the end product looks like. This will give the trainee a clear idea of what has to be accomplished as a result of the one-to-one training or coaching experience. Furthermore, it will allow trainees to judge their own performance against what they expect to be an acceptable standard.

For objective setting to be a valuable technique in a training context the following conditions must be met:

- objectives must be within the trainee's ability to achieve them;
- feedback on how well the objective is being met is given to the trainee at appropriate intervals;
- individuals are given specific challenging objectives rather than modest objectives or no objectives at all, or simply encouraged to 'do your best'.

Apart from telling the trainee about the overall learning objectives at the outset, the trainer can influence the trainee's ongoing attitudes and motivation towards the learning programme by setting or agreeing a series of shorter term or interim objectives with him or her. This process of progressive learning objectives will enable the trainer to monitor closely the trainee's achievement and, to a certain extent, to adjust the organization of the instructional or coaching programme to meet individual needs.

Providing a Meaningful Context

Apart from stimulating the trainee's motivation by the setting of objectives, the trainer needs to arrange the learning environment to maintain alertness throughout the training sessions. Those sessions that are run as on-the-job training, are already placed in the context of the work environment and little has to be done to make it more stimulating. However, some aspects of training have to be taught as discrete items and may not be directly related to what has gone before or what follows. For example, a training session which involves recording code numbers on record cards or on a computer may not seem very meaningful until it is explained that the code numbers refer to drugs used in medicine and that they relate to the control of prescriptions for an individual's treatment. Giving an overview of the task and showing its relationship to other tasks and activities provides a more meaningful context in which the learning can take place.

Another way in which a meaningful context can be provided is by simulating an environment which resembles, as closely as is possible, the real working conditions. The example of a flight simulator readily comes to mind but less sophisticated means can be used such as taking a motoring organization mechanic to a wet and cold location to detect and repair a fault on the engine of a motor car.

Directing Attention

There will be occasions when the trainer has to draw the trainee's attention to certain distinctive or critical features of the task or skill to be learned. These features may be associated with any of the six senses: vision, hearing, touch, smell, taste and what is called proprioceptive sense (this sense relates to the position and movement of the body, eg, balance).

Learning to cook, for example, could potentially emphasize the use of vision, smell and taste. On the other hand learning to tune a car might rely quite heavily on hearing. In this case the trainer might start and stop or vary the critical sound of the engine to get the learner to pay attention or notice it.

Pictures and Demonstrations

An old Chinese proverb, now often quoted by trainers, serves to highlight the importance of pictures and demonstrations:

I hear and I forget
I see and I remember
I do and I understand

Pictures and demonstrations can provide trainees with a mental plan which will help them to remember the sequence of actions or steps involved in procedural or manual skills. It is worth bearing in mind that in demonstrations, actions speak louder than words. Therefore, when critical actions or behaviours are being demonstrated, the trainer should keep the verbal commentary to a minimum to prevent the learner becoming distracted by being 'overloaded' with words. If the trainer has to talk during a demonstration then they should stick to key points.

Human Modelling

This is closely associated with demonstrations and will be looked at in more detail in Chapter 4 in relation to social skills training. It is sufficient to say at this stage that for human modelling to be effective the model used must:

— appeal to, and have credibility for, the trainee;
— demonstrate clearly the suitable course or choice of action;
— be seen to be, or have been, rewarded for behaving in the desired way, ie, is worth doing.

Verbal Instruction

Verbal instruction can be used in training and instructional contexts in a number of ways:

33

- to communicate background information, ideas, etc, that provide the meaningful context in which to fit any new learning;
- to explain concepts, rules, principles and theories that provide the necessary foundation for, or follow-up to, learning procedural, manual and social skills;
- to be essential in supporting other learning principles and conditions.

If the trainer is to ensure that verbal instructions are clearly understood then sentences must be short and uncomplicated. Long, complex sentences are likely to be misunderstood and lead to confusion.

Guidance, Prompting and Cueing

These terms are very similar in that they are all used to direct the learner at times when they are actually involved in doing something and the trainer feels that there is a need to give some help. Although they are discussed separately for means of explanation, their function is the same.

- Guidance can be given in two ways. It can be an abbreviated form of demonstration by showing the trainee the right way of doing something such as how to hold a tool properly before they actually use it. Also, guidance is used when mistakes could occur and the trainee is alerted to the need to take care or to work slowly. It is best used in training manual and social skills.

  It is particularly important to provide guidance in the early phases of learning complex tasks. Errors that are made at this time are likely to be repeated and subsequently learning resources have to be devoted to unlearning those early mistakes. It is also important to prevent errors occurring in training where serious safety problems or damage to equipment might result.

  However, there may be circumstances in which allowing errors to be committed might be beneficial as more may be learned from making mistakes than from making correct responses.

  Having said all this, it is worth remembering that the trainer has to exercise some balance in the amount of guidance given. Observing the trainee's reaction to guidance will give some indication of how much it is welcomed and needed and how far there may be a danger of boredom and demotivation because the trainee may feel that he or she does not have sufficient independence and control over their own learning.

- Prompting is more applicable to learning verbal material associated with procedural tasks. After some initial learning of information the trainee may be required to recall it and is helped to do this by being 'prompted' by the trainer. Skilful questioning of the trainee may also act as a form of prompting, leading to the correct response or action. As with guidance, prompting appears to be particularly effective in the initial phase of learning.

— A trainee's learning can sometimes be speeded up by the trainer providing or highlighting easily identifiable and easily remembered cues which 'trigger' the correct response or sequence of actions. For example, in some forms of social skills training such as selling, the trainee's attention can be directed towards cues such as a client's facial or oral expressions, tone of voice, etc, that will help the trainee to interpret particular social situations and then to behave appropriately. Skilful salesmen are good at picking up and responding to buying 'signals' or cues.

Practice and Rehearsal

Ultimately it is the trainee who does the learning and he or she has to participate and be actively involved if this process is to be effective. Practice and rehearsal are two of the important activities that trainees must engage in, under the influence and direction of the trainer so as to acquire new knowledge and skills.

There are two initial conditions that need to be present if practice is going to 'make perfect'. First, the learner must want to achieve an improvement in performance and second, that feedback is provided, on an on-going basis during and at the end of the practice period.

Similarly, for rehearsal to be an effective method of ensuring verbal or procedural material is remembered, it must involve the trainee in active retrieval and recall of the material during the training or coaching session. This form of activity is important because:

— it requires active participation by the learner and this helps to maintain attention and interest;
— active recall gives the learner an opportunity to practise on the material;
— being informed about accuracy will indicate to the learner what he or she does or does not know and should help them to direct and to allocate subsequent effort and time.

Distribution of practice

The trainer will need to consider whether practice should be all at once ('massed') or spread over several sessions ('distributed'). Although it is difficult to provide absolutely conclusive guidelines the following should be borne in mind:

- in learning manual skills, distributed practice is usually more effective than massed practice both in the learning phase and in terms of retention;
- when the material to be learned does not make immediate sense to trainees or cannot be associated with what they already know or are skilled in, it will be more difficult to learn in a massed session as opposed to a series of sessions;
- the ideal time interval between practice sessions and the length of the session itself will depend on the nature of the task or skill to be learned and on the trainee's personality, previous learning experience, etc (see sections on Individual Differences). If the interval is too long then forgetting may become a problem and relearning or a 'warm-up' period may be necessary. On the other hand, if the rest interval is too short then trainees may become bored or suffer from mental or physical fatigue.

Imagining and Reflection

Mental practice can be a way of improving a trainee's ability to learn manual and social skills. The trainee would first observe a demonstration of the skill in question, then have some initial experience of it, and finally be encouraged to imagine the relevant skilled movements, behaviours, etc. Naturally, this procedure would have to be used in conjunction with other forms of learning.

Reflection, as a form of mental rehearsal, may lead the trainee to 'reveal' or raise pertinent questions about the training content. The answer to these questions, given either by the trainer or by other means, may then speed up subsequent learning.

Discovery Learning and Exploration

Provided the consequences for the trainees of making errors are not serious or harmful, they may learn a great deal by being allowed to 'have a go' on their own, with little or no involvement by the trainer. It is important that the work pieces or situations to be tackled are chosen carefully so they are potentially within the trainee's scope to complete successfully. It might be very disheartening and demotivating if a trainee was asked to learn tasks that are clearly beyond his or her ability. Some form of de-briefing session should take place between trainee and trainer after the 'discovery' experience so that the trainer can confirm that the right lessons have been learned.

Sometimes a less circumscribed means of discovery can be of benefit to the trainees. If they are simply allowed to explore the training situation and 'play with' the equipment then, safety considerations permitting, greater interest may be generated resulting in more inquisitiveness and ultimately wider learning. However, it must be emphasized that discovery should not be confused with 'being thrown in at the deep end'. Discovery learning is monitored and controlled by the trainer, it is structured and it is planned. Nothing that the trainee does should pass unnoticed by the trainer.

Feedback, Knowledge of Results and Reinforcement

Trainees need to know how well they are doing at all stages in their training if they are going to learn effectively and improve their performance. Feedback can be provided by the trainer and may focus on how well a trainee performs a particular task. Alternatively, the trainee can be directed to look out for cues and information that allow him or her to judge how effectively he or she is progressing. When learning to play a musical instrument the learner will hear, see and sometimes feel how well he or she is performing.

The trainer must be concerned with two important features of feedback: how much to give and how specific to make it. Too much specific feedback in the early stages may not necessarily lead to improvements in performance. To 'overload' the trainee with too much detailed information about performance may only serve to confuse and may also have a depressing effect on the trainee's motivation.

The general recommendation on feedback would seem to be to give the trainee a small amount early on, increase the amount and specific detail as the trainee improves and then withdraw it gradually as the skills to be learned become more established, before finally excluding it altogether. When giving feedback the trainer must not ignore the trainee's emotional needs. Some form of emotional reward, such as 'well done', should follow effective performance of parts, or the whole, of the task. However, this form of reinforcement must not be overdone, otherwise the trainer's sincerity may be brought into question. Furthermore the trainee must not become overly dependent on emotional support from the trainer. This is because the trainee's confidence and consequently their performance may be adversely affected when this kind of support is withdrawn. On the other hand praise or reassurance as an ongoing process may be necessary and important when progress is depressingly slow or non-existent and the trainee needs to be urged on.

Principles, Conditions and Types of Training

The principles, conditions and features of learning which have been covered so far are not all equally applicable to the different types of one-to-one instruction, ie, procedural, manual or social, and to coaching. Figure 2.1 sets out those which generally are most appropriate to these different categories of training.

Learning Principles and Conditions	Manual	Procedural	Social	Coaching
Sequencing	*	*	*	*
Whole or Part	*	*	*	*
Setting objectives & Sub-objectives	*	*	*	*
Meaningful context	*	*	*	*
Directing attention	*	*	*	*
Pictures & Demonstrations	*	*	* (Demonstration)	*
Human Modelling	-	-	*	*
Verbal Instruction	*	*	*	*
Guidance Prompting & Cueing	* (Guidance)	* (Prompting)	* (Cueing)	*
Practice & Rehearsal	* (Practice)	* (Practice)	* (Rehearsal)	* (Rehearsal)
Imagining & Reflection	* (Imagining)	* (Imagining)	*	*
Distribution of Practice	* (Spaced)	* (Massed)	* (Spaced)	*
Discovery & Exploration	*	-	*	*
Feedback, K of R & Reinforcement	*	*	*	*

Figure 2.1 *Learning principles and conditions used for the manual, procedural and social skills.*

Individual Differences

The principles and conditions of learning which have been described provide general guidelines to trainers to help them to plan and design one-to-one instructional or coaching sessions. However, it must be appreciated that not all individuals will react or respond to these principles and conditions in the same way. Therefore, some flexibility needs to be used in their introduction and application. Such flexibility cannot be applied sensibly unless the trainer has some knowledge of individual differences. This knowledge is important for two very good reasons. First, it may help to explain why certain individuals are not behaving or responding as might be expected (ie, in a similar way to other trainees). Second, it could offer an opportunity to cater for trainees' needs when something is known about their style, attitudes and preferences. Five important factors that illustrate the link between individual differences, learning principles and conditions, and one-to-one instruction or coaching, are age, levels of intelligence and ability, emotional state, learning style and learner maturity.

Age

There are a number of important differences between young and older trainees. Generally speaking, the older individual learns more slowly and has more difficulty 'grasping' new material than his younger counterpart. Furthermore, if the older person makes a mistake early in training then the error is likely to persist and correcting it becomes more difficult. However, all is not 'doom and gloom'; there are a number of suggestions or hints on how to manage training or coaching sessions to compensate for some of the difficulties that older learners experience:

- Avoid, where possible, instruction that relies on the need for memorizing large amounts of information.
- Ensure that the learner has had a chance to show that one task has been mastered before moving on to the next.
- Make sure that errors are corrected as soon as possible because they tend to persist with the older learner; ideally try to ensure errors do not occur at all.
- Where possible, try to instruct in meaningful 'whole' parts of a task rather than smaller stages that do not seem connected. For example, in training someone to pack a fragile object for transporting by road, it would be more appropriate to teach the whole process rather than to break it up into separate stages

such as making up a box, cutting paper to size, handling different protective materials, etc.

— Provide variety by changing or modifying the method of instruction; repetition using the same method can tire the older trainee.

— Use longer uninterrupted learning periods than might be used with younger learners; interrupted or short sessions may cause forgetfulness in the older learner.

— Let the older trainee proceed at his or her own pace and let them compete against themselves rather than against targets achieved by others.

— The discovery method of instruction can be helpful on occasions provided that the tasks are carefully graded in difficulty.

— With complex tasks get the older trainee to learn by stages which gradually increase in complexity.

— Avoid formal time limits for the completion of different phases of the task and do not use formal tests of progress and achievement.

— If a task has to be learned in parts because of its complexity or breadth then employ the cumulative part method, ie, a, a + b, a + b + c, etc. For example, if we were teaching someone to play a complex piece of music, they could be taught to play one bar correctly and then the next bar before playing the two bars together. Then a third bar could be added. The same technique is used by actors to learn their lines.

It must not be assumed that there is a standard or 'clone-like' older person. There is a greater disparity in intelligence and intellectual ability amongst older people than the younger group. Therefore, in the light of this, some of the above suggestions could be modified; for instance allowing the older trainee to proceed at his or her own pace.

Levels of Intelligence and Ability

Learning principles and tactics should be varied depending on the ability or intelligence level of the trainee. The higher-ability individuals or those who have had a more academic education are more likely to be able to work from general principles to concrete situations and, depending on the complexity of the task, cope with learning a task as a whole. For example it may be more appropriate to teach the principles and theoretical aspects of electricity to those with more academic experience before demonstrating and practising wiring a house. With those with less academic experience it would be better to tackle the practical aspects first. On the other hand, for the less-able trainee or slower learner the trainer should:

- use small learning steps and employ the cumulative part method;
- proceed from concrete examples to general principles;
- avoid unstructured training situations as the slow or low-ability learners are more easily distracted by irrelevant information;
- keep explanations brief as the slow learner may have difficulty understanding long, expansive instruction;
- employ short learning sessions which will prevent possible boredom and discouragement;
- make sure that there is plenty of opportunity for practice.

Emotional State

An individual's emotional state may influence how and what he or she learns. Anxiety, fear of failure and lack of confidence are the sorts of feeling experienced by some trainees that can badly affect their motivation and willingness to learn. In order to counteract these barriers the trainer may need to:

- allow the trainee to control the pace of the session – only nudging them forward in a gentle manner, eg, 'Do you feel confident now to move on to the next step?';
- structure the session quite tightly and avoid using the discovery method;
- set more easily attainable goals and do not make comparisons between the trainee and other learners;
- give plenty of guidance and emotional support and give feedback on progress as often as possible;
- reassure the trainees when there are periods of little or no progress, which are fairly natural in most learning situations (see Learning Curves and Plateaux on page 44);
- divide up the instructional period into short, easily managed stages;
- ensure that the trainees are not left to practise for long periods on their own because if they get into difficulties they will need to be given assistance quite promptly.

Of course, individuals who are over-confident or arrogant may need to be brought down to earth with one or two 'special', safe but chastening experiences.

Learning Style

The idea of learning style refers to the fact that individuals differ in their inclination to learn from different activities or approaches. For instance, some people like to carry out practical exercises at an early stage of training and will be prepared to learn by their mistakes. Others like to watch demonstrations and receive explanations first before reflecting on the content and assessing its relevance and importance to their own circumstances. In the United Kingdom, Honey and Mumford (1986) have identified and defined four basic learning styles:

Activists. Enjoy the here and now; dominated by immediate experiences, they tend to revel in the short-term crisis, and firefighting activities. They thrive on the challenge of new experiences but are relatively bored with implementation and longer-term consolidation. They are the life and soul of the party.

Reflectors. Like to stand back and ponder on experiences and observe them from different perspectives. They collect data and analyse them before coming to any conclusions. They like to consider all possible angles and implications before making a move, so they tend to be cautious. They actually enjoy observing other people in action and often take a back seat.

Theorists. Are keen on basic assumptions, principles, theories, models and systems thinking. They prize rationality and logic. They tend to be detached, analytical, and are unhappy with subjective or ambiguous experiences. They like to assemble disparate facts into coherent theories. They like to make things tidy and fit them into rational schemes.

Pragmatists. Positively search out new ideas and take the first opportunity to experiment with applications. They are the sort of people who return from courses brimming with new ideas that they want to try out. They respond to problems and opportunities 'as a challenge' (the Activists probably would not recognize them as problems and opportunities).

Recognizing the predominant preferred style of trainees can have implications for the kind of approach that trainers adopt. This is particularly relevant with regard to how activists and reflectors learn best in one-to-one instructional situations and to how pragmatists learn best from coaching programmes.

Activists seem to learn more easily when they can get involved immediately in short 'here and now' practical activities and when there is a variety of things to cope with; they are not put off by being 'thrown in at the deep end'. Activists do not learn well when they are required simply to observe and not to be involved or when they are required to listen to theoretical explanations. Highly-structured massed practice sessions, ie, where an activity is practised over and over again, would also not be liked by the activist.

On the other hand, reflectors probably learn best when they are allowed to watch, observe or listen and then think over or review what has taken place. They certainly need to 'look before they leap' and to be given plenty of time for preparation. Being 'thrown' into situations without warning would also lead to an adverse reaction from reflectors.

In coaching situations, pragmatists need to work with developments or techniques that have an obvious practical 'pay off'; they must concentrate on practical job-related issues. For the pragmatist the content of the coaching session must not be theoretical but clearly related to reality.

Ideally, an individual's learning style preference could be assessed in a reasonably objective way by means of a questionnaire prior to the beginning of a series of one-to-one or coaching sessions. The benefits of this for the trainer are that:

- it would help trainers to design sessions that fit in with the predominant styles of the trainees;
- if the results of the questionnaire were 'fed back' to the trainees it could help them to appreciate the difficulties they might experience with the training methods that, out of necessity, have to be used in their training;
- it would identify for trainers those individuals who may need special attention because the learning style contrasts greatly with the methods that the trainer needs to use;
- it could allow trainers to put into perspective the trainees' observations and comments about the training content and approach.

However, even without such structured questionnaire information, trainers could probably make a general assessment of trainees' styles based on pre-training interviews with them which might explore their educational or occupational background and previous training or learning experiences.

Learner Maturity

Another individual difference that the trainer should take into account is the 'maturity of the learner'. Stuart and Holmes (1982) suggest that maturity in this context is not referring to the trainee's age but rather to his or her:

- capacity to set high but attainable learning goals;
- willingness and ability to take responsibility for their learning;
- educational and previous experiences.

For immature learners the trainer must try to ensure that they can 'walk before they can run'. 'Pushing' trainees too fast is likely to have negative effects on their learning time and their motivation. Initially, with these kinds of trainee the trainer needs to be persuasive, in control and to be more directive. As the trainee matures the trainer should then become less structured in his or her approach and concentrate more on guiding, advising and supporting. With mature trainees, trainers must definitely avoid trying to 'teach them to suck eggs'. If they adopt this role they will be seen as over-structured and patronising. The mature trainee will respond better to a more participative, challenging and collaborative relationship.

Additional Considerations

In addition to the principles and conditions of learning and the individual differences already covered there are a number of other factors that need to be taken into account. These are learning curves and plateaux, retention and forgetting, and transfer of training.

Learning Curves and Plateaux

Trainers must appreciate that progress in learning a new skill may not be consistent. In some tasks the general pattern may mean that most trainees make rapid early progress followed by relatively marginal or minor improvements as they begin to gain increased competence. In this kind of situation the trainer may need to be more encouraging towards the end of a training session or series of sessions so as to 'lift' the trainee's motivation. This could also be done by introducing some alternative stimulating activity so that the trainee goes back to the main task refreshed. The converse pattern of learning may also exist for some complex and difficult tasks: slow initial progress followed by acceleration as the number of training sessions increases. Not surprisingly, the trainees' motivation may be fairly low in the first stages which further serves to hold up their performance. In these circumstances the trainer probably will need to give more guidance and encouragement early on.

Another familiar and characteristic pattern observed in some learning is referred to as the 'learning plateau'. This is a period in the learning process when no obvious progress is being made. This is often experienced by people when they are learning to drive a car. Initially, progress is fast as the basic skills are learned and then there seems to be a period of little or no progress and sometimes learners feel that they have actually got worse. Then everything seems to come together and progress becomes more noticable (see Figure 2.2).

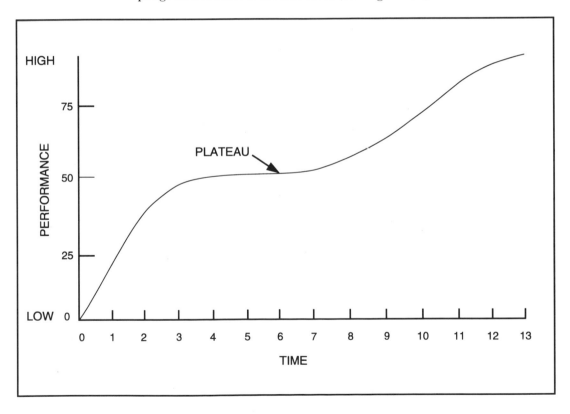

Figure 2.2 *The learning plateau*

By introducing some form of incentive or changing the trainees' activity for a short period they may move through the plateau fairly quickly. Early introduction of more accurate and detailed feedback might bring about a similar result. Furthermore, reassuring the trainee that the learning plateau is a fairly normal experience may prevent a motivational 'hang up'.

Retention and Forgetting

Forgetting what was originally learned is a common enough experience. However, it is often vital to ensure that skills and knowledge learned in training are retained and made full use of in the work situation, otherwise there could be serious or even disastrous consequences. This may be difficult to achieve if there is little or no opportunity to employ the knowledge and skills immediately or on a frequent basis in the work context. There are a number of suggestions or procedures that can be used which could prevent or minimize the retention problem.

- Introduce the use of a job aid. This can act as a form of *aide-mémoire* back in the work place. A job aid is any form of printed document containing verbal or pictorial material kept in the place of work which can be used as a memory jogger or as a procedural guide for a difficult, complex or infrequently performed task.
- Use distributed rather than massed practice sessions.
- Train to produce over-learning in the trainee, ie, train to a level of performance above that which is strictly needed to achieve the training objectives.
- Encourage the trainees to engage in mental practice or rehearsal when they return to their work locations.
- Make the training as meaningful as possible by linking it with the trainees' previous knowledge and experience and by organizing it and sequencing it to make initial learning easier.
- Try to make sure that the way the training and coaching sessions are run motivates the trainees, stimulates their interest and is not an experience they would rather forget.

Transfer of Training

Positive transfer, in relation to one-to-one instruction or coaching, refers to the ability of trainees to apply what they have learned when they are 'let loose' to work on their own. If the trainees are unable to do this then it would bring into question the learning conditions and tactics employed in the instructional or coaching sessions. There are several recommendations that trainers should consider applying in order to help along the process of positive transfer.

- Where feasible, make the training situation as similar as possible to the work situation in terms of physical conditions (ie, equipment, surroundings, etc) and psychological conditions (ie, task and social demands, etc). In the latter case the trainer would probably need to 'build up' to these real conditions over time.
- Give trainees plenty of opportunity to practise and rehearse the task or skill, to the point of over-learning.
- Introduce the trainees to a variety of examples such as pieces of work or situations to tackle, or relevant conditions in which to practise the skill.
- Ensure that the critical features of the work conditions are drawn to the attention of the trainee during training.
- Avoid putting trainees through rote-learning sessions as this tends to discourage transfer.
- Show the value of the training to the work setting; the trainees' perception of its value and his or her strong motivation to succeed may carry over to the job, which, in turn, will have a positive impact on transfer.
- In the post-training situation set goals for or with the trainees and give objective and timely feedback.

Conclusion

This chapter has set out some general guidelines and considerations that the trainer and coach should take into account in one-to-one instructional or coaching situations. However, these guidelines and considerations must not be applied in a mechanistic, unthinking and unintelligent manner. It is better for trainers to find out what works best in particular circumstances with certain types of instructional material and target populations.

3 Preparing to Train

▷   SUMMARY   ◁

In this chapter you will learn about:
- How to prepare training programmes and individual one-to-one training sessions.
- The use of check-lists, family trees and procedural guides.
- The structure of training objectives.

It has been mentioned already that a large part of the investment in training is allowing time for preparation. Trainers and line managers often fail to appreciate the amount of preparation that needs to be done. It is only when trainers have been guided through the stages of preparation and have experienced its value that they feel some justification in asking for time to do their jobs properly.

Preparation is in two stages. The longer-term preparation demands the greater amount of time and the shorter-term preparation is undertaken just before a training session begins. This chapter will concentrate on the longer-term preparation; the shorter-term will be discussed in the context of the one-to-one training model in Chapter 4.

A useful starting point is to consider preparation as a non-mathematical equation:

Who

  Where

Why   +   = How

  When

What

By using this as a guide, we can pay attention to all the relevant factors relating to preparation and also make decisions about how training can be best presented. The first group of factors – who, why and what – are usually looked at simultaneously; we cannot keep our thoughts rigidly in separate compartments. However, by placing 'who' at the top of the list, emphasis is placed on the most important person in the process, namely, the person who has to be trained. The word 'why' directs us to think in terms of the training needs of the individual and, having established what they are, to find out 'what' they need to learn. The words 'where' and 'when' represent the logistic considerations of environment as well as equipment and facilities, plus how much time is available for preparation and conducting the training. All of this helps to make the decision on how best to train and therefore each aspect of the equation needs to be looked at in some detail.

Who is to be Trained?

The person who has to be trained is the starting point for preparation. There is always a danger of placing too much emphasis on the content of training at the expense of the trainee and then, when training fails or is less effective than was expected, blame is placed on the ability or capacity of the trainee. There are a number of areas about which questions can be asked to build up a profile of the trainee which will make it much easier to prepare the training.

Work History in the Organization

It should not be taken for granted that all those who need to be trained are inexperienced newcomers. The reason for their need to be trained could be because new equipment, new procedures or new products are being introduced; it could be that they have to retrain in new skills because their current skills are no longer required. All of this could add up to a considerable amount of experience of the organization and the way in which it operates. It follows that it would be wasteful, if not annoying, for the trainee if the trainer decided to teach basic skills and procedures which were already well-known and well-practised. However, for someone with limited experience it is more likely that there would be a need to teach some of the basic elements of the job. For example, if a large agricultural or forestry organization bought a new vehicle with a number of attachments or facilities on it, the experienced worker who has been trained on other vehicles may need only to be trained on a new ditch digging attachment whereas the less-experienced worker may need to learn how to use a hedge cutter and a circular-saw attachment as well.

Work history can also give pointers towards motivation. Some staff may be having to learn new skills because the jobs that they have been doing for years have become redundant and they may feel some resentment about having to retrain. It might also mean that they will have to 'unlearn' some of the practices which have become second nature to them in order to develop new ones. This could involve the trainer in having to progress slowly and in small stages. On the other hand the trainees could be young and enthusiastic 'high flyers' who are eager to be trained.

Time and Progress in Current Job or when Due to Take Up Duties

Planning and delivering training at the 'right' time is always a problem. Trainers may not always be available when training is needed and those who need to be trained may have to try as best as they can to do the job until training can be provided. The trainer also faces that strange situation where line managers say that they cannot release staff to be trained because they need them, albeit untrained, to do the job. Close liaison and forward planning between trainers and line managers can help to avert these kinds of situation.

When someone has been occupied for some time in a job, it is quite likely that they will have learned some tasks on their own initiative, by trial and error or with the assistance of a co-worker. In the process, they could have learned some bad habits as well as correct procedures. The trainer needs to find out exactly what the trainee has learned. It could be that there is nothing more to do than to verify that the job holder is competent and has succeeded in learning the job by him or herself. On the other hand, and particularly where bad habits have formed, a programme of unlearning and relearning would have to be prepared. When a trainee has not yet taken up the job for which training is needed or a new procedure does not come into force for some time, care should be taken not to train too soon. Learning is reinforced by practice and if there is too big a time gap between training and applying what has been learned, the trainee is likely to forget. For example, if a wages clerk is taught how to calculate stoppages on staff pay-slips and then doesn't become involved in that work for several weeks, we should not be surprised if errors are made.

Ideally, training should be followed immediately by putting into practice what has been learned. It is always important to ensure that arrangements for the prompt application of knowledge and skills are included in the training plan. This will also help to avoid those situations where staff are nominated for training in the mistaken belief that it will 'do them good' and that 'they are bound to get something out of it'.

What Previous Training has been Undertaken and When?

Knowledge about previous training that the trainee has undertaken often serves as an indicator as to how they may approach and progress in subsequent training programmes. Those who have been trained recently are more likely to be able to adapt to learning situations than those who have not been involved in training for some time or those who may never have been trained in any structured way at all. Those who are limited in their experience of participating in training activities could have a fear of the unknown, an anxiety that they might not be successful, a dread of showing their limitations or unhappy memories of previous attempts at learning. For example, a storeman in a motor components factory may have to learn how to use a computer system to control stock. If his previous experience of learning had been when he was at school and if that experience had not been a happy one, it could be expected that he would be somewhat wary of being trained. This is not an unfamiliar situation in changing organizations which demand new skills of their established workforce.

Those who are used to being trained are more likely to have developed their learning skills and to adapt more easily to learning situations. They feel more confident, they know that making errors is part of the learning process and that the trainer does not expect instant success. In short, they feel more secure in a training environment because they know how to establish a rapport with the trainer and how they are expected to behave. They know the ground rules and are likely to learn more quickly and more easily.

Is Training Part of Induction?

If the training we are about to undertake is part of an induction programme we need to find out how far the trainee is into the programme. Induction training does not always follow a set sequence and as trainers we should make sure that we do not make assumptions about what has been taught already or what will have been taught by the time that it comes to our turn. Even then it is worthwhile to check this again at the beginning of our first session in case plans have had to change. Induction training usually includes basic skills, organizational knowledge, conditions of service, etc. Our training becomes more difficult if something has been taught in the wrong order. For example the trainer would find it necessary to re-structure a session if a storeman arrived for training in preparing items for despatch without first having been taught how to interpret item coding on invoices.

Is the Trainee a Recent School Leaver?

School leavers need to be catered for with care. Many of them leave their first employment within a year and the reason most frequently given is 'nobody showed me what to do', or lack of training. School leavers have to undergo a period of adjustment which, for some of them, can be quite stressful. They have to adjust to the world of work and often do not know how to behave in their new environment. Guidance is needed on how to address their fellow workers and their seniors. They are likely to be unsure about the relationship they should form with their trainers, having only experienced learning in a school or college environment. There is also the likelihood of underestimating the naïvety of school leavers when they enter the world of work. A popular pastime over the years in many working environments has been to take advantage of such naïvety by playing tricks on newcomers such as sending them for 'a tin of elbow grease', 'a tin of striped paint', 'a left-handed screwdriver', 'a long wait', and many others. The joke always seems to work and is an illustration that we cannot make any assumptions about their level of familiarity with the organization or the subject matter that we intend to teach.

What Sort of Person is the Trainee?

Whether the trainee is lively or reserved, anxious or confident, willing to 'have a go' or tends to hang back, are features which help us as trainers to prepare ourselves and our approach. It comes as something of a surprise if we are not prepared for the over-confident trainee who thinks that he or she knows it all and that there is nothing that we can do for them. Other facets of personality that might be noted are those described in the consideration of individual differences in Chapter 2.

Is the Trainee Returning to Work after a Career Break?

This situation is becoming a feature of the workforce in many organizations. People return to work after varying periods of absence after having brought up a family or on deciding to return from early retirement. A careful assessment of their training needs should be made to ensure that they are fully up-to-date with procedures, processes, equipment and materials which may well have changed even after only a short period of absence.

It is also useful to think about their personal needs on returning to work. Some may be anxious or even fearful of any changes that may have occurred and whether they will be able to cope.

How Old is the Trainee?

It has been found that people often find difficulty with learning as they grow older. One cannot attribute precise ages to particular learning difficulties but in general terms there are some which become noticeable as people age. The more common of these situations are:

- when tasks involve the need for short-term memory;
- when there is 'interference' from other activities or other learning;
- when learning is abstract or unrelated to realities as might be found in concepts relating to supervisory or managerial skills;
- when there is a need to 'unlearn' old skills and procedures in which the trainee is well-practiced;
- when there is a lack of confidence;
- when learning becomes mentally passive.

Strategies which can be used to overcome these potential problems were introduced in Chapter 2.

Does the Trainee have any Special Needs?

Many more people with disabilities are being employed to perform tasks which in the past have been the domain of only the able-bodied. New technology has assisted greatly in this respect; for example, staff with sight impairments are able to use word processors with the assistance of enhancements which include speech synthesisers. The trainer needs to know the nature of any disability that trainees might have and any special equipment or facilities that they need. People with disabilities are not usually embarrassed by discussing their disability; it is more likely that the trainer will feel awkward. Rather than 'skating around' the issue it is far better to ask straight out if there are any arrangements that need to be made for them.

Where do We Get the Information from?

There are a number of sources from which information about the trainee can be obtained. These include the trainees, personnel records, line managers and supervisors. In many instances line managers and supervisors are the trainers and either initiate the training activities themselves or are directed by their immediate superiors. To avoid confusion, the word 'sponsor' is used to refer to situations where the person who acts as the trainer has been tasked by someone who is senior to them in the organization.

Getting information from sponsors serves a two-fold purpose. Firstly, the sponsors should know their staff well enough to be able to have much of the information that is needed at their finger-tips and should be able to access other details from records with comparative ease. This saves a considerable amount of time.

Apart from being a readily available source of information, the additional advantage of referring to the sponsor is to gain or confirm their commitment to the training and to negotiate such resources as time, materials and equipment in order to conduct the training properly. In fact, the trainer should always make contact with the sponsor in order to achieve this second objective. Very often, one-to-one trainers have to conduct the training whilst performing their normal duties and therefore sponsors must expect a slower operational performance from the trainer if sufficient time is going to be given to training.

Access to personnel records may be limited, particularly for junior members of staff. When this is the case it is not a bad idea to have a set of standard questions written out which can be handed to the supervisor in advance. Many training departments make use of a training log which the trainee retains and which is signed when each new piece of training or each revision session has been completed. Others make use of training record cards. Both of these documents are useful sources of information for the trainer.

However, if these sources do not exist or are difficult to tap into – and to be realistic, not all sponsors are as approachable or as helpful as we might like them to be – then we can speak directly to the trainee.

By speaking informally with trainees before the training begins we can build the foundation of a sound working relationship. It makes it an easier start when trainees know the person who is going to train them and it is even easier when they like them. It can also help to allay any fears or apprehension and clarify any pre-course preparation that may have to be done. The trainer can make a fair, albeit subjective, assessment of what level of performance the trainee has achieved to date and how he or she is likely to react and progress during training.

These findings can be noted either on paper or mentally depending on how many trainees the one-to-one trainer may have to train and how good his or her memory is. Examples of written notes are shown in Figures 3.1 and 3.2.

TRAINEE   *Grace Fox*   *32 Years*

- Worked in Accounts for 10 years before leaving to have a family.

- Returning after six years.

- Previous experience on paper-based system.

- So far had 2 weeks of learning keyboard skills and making very good progress - quick to learn, willing to ask questions.

- A pleasant personality, a little reserved to begin with but more confident now that she has made a few friends.

- TRAINING NEEDED - Complete Part 6 of Staff Induction Programme.

  - All sections in Accounts Training Manual.

- TRAINING STARTS - 4 June.

Figure 3.1 *Example 1, pre-training trainee profile*

TRAINEE   *Ralph Lyons   18 Years*

● Left school at 16 years with low grade exam passes.

● Began work at a Supermarket but left because it was boring.

● Been with us for 4 weeks employed in reception and cleaning used cars for sales staff. Has worked hard.

● Sometimes noisy and a bit of a 'know it all'.

● Has own car which he claims he services and repairs but seems to have some bad habits with servicing and doesn't really know much about repairs.

● TRAINING NEEDED - Part 1 Servicing petrol driven engines.

       - Note - monitor to ensure no bad practice.

● TRAINING STARTS - 11 October.

Figure 3.2 *Example 2, pre-training trainee profile*

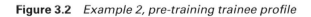

Why is Training Needed?

So far the emphasis has been on *who* is going to be trained and how knowing something about them helps trainers in their preparation. A factor closely related to *who* is *why* they need to be trained. The natural assumption would be that they had a training need. This exists when there is a current or an anticipated shortfall in performance or when performance could be improved to result in increased productivity or a higher quality of service. Another over-riding factor is that the increased productivity or higher quality of service should be linked to the organization's objectives.

However, not everyone who presents themselves for training is aware of their needs and, in fact, many do not have needs as they have been described above. Some staff are trained for the wrong reasons; they may be currently under-employed, they may be a nuisance in the work place or it may be a case of the unit or department improving its training statistics. While this kind of situation may seem far-fetched, there are many examples of it happening. Those who do need training do not always know why. Ideally, they should have been briefed by their sponsors in advance of beginning of their training. It is not wise to assume that this has always been done and part of the trainer's preparation should be to remind sponsors that the trainee needs to be briefed. Naturally, when the trainer makes a point of meeting the trainee as part of his preliminary preparation, this kind of problem can be avoided. There is nothing worse than trying to train someone who doesn't know why he or she is being trained and how that training will be used subsequently. The trainer should not be expected to play the sponsor's or the line manager's role in motivating the trainee and it is always worthwhile to ask sponsors how the trainees have or will be briefed in respect of the following:

- What the aim of the training is and what it will cover.
- How the training fits into the trainee's career or employment plan.
- What the value of the training will be to the department or section, etc, where the trainee is employed.
- Preparation that may have to be undertaken before training.
- Additional work that may have to be done in the trainee's own time, such as reading.
- What will be expected in terms of improved performance or additional skills after the training.
- Any worries that the trainee may have about the forthcoming training.

- What support and monitoring will be available from the line manager and the trainer during training.
- Confirmation that there will be a debriefing with the trainee on completion of training.

What will the Training Consist of?

Having clarified who has to be trained and why they need to be trained, the next factor to be looked at is *what* they need to be trained in. Finding out about the trainee will have given a reasonable assessment of what training needs to be done but it is quite likely that other needs will emerge during training. These additional needs should be built into the training plan as they arise. Much of the planning of the content will depend on the size of the organization, the diversity of its work, the size or existence of the training department, the organization's approach to training and its resourcing of training. At best the one-to-one trainer is part of a structured and planned training system and at worst, he or she is in a 'Nellie' situation with little or no support or understanding on the part of the organization. The extent to which the one-to-one trainer will be involved in content planning will depend upon a combination of the factors discussed above. The reasons for making sure that the content is assessed properly become clear when the costs of too much or too little training are considered:

Costs of too much training:

- More training being organized than is needed.
- Training takes longer than it needs to.
- More trainers, equipment and materials are being used than are necessary.
- Job dissatisfaction if the trainee's expectations of the job are not met.
- Skills and procedures are forgotten if they are taught too soon.

Costs of too little training:

- Additional time and resources have to be given to further training.
- Error rates and wastage have to be absorbed until further training is undertaken.
- Low morale on the part of former trainee possibly leading to the trainee leaving.

If the one-to-one trainer is working to the directions of a training department, then it is likely that there will be training kits or check-lists to work to. The task of the trainer then becomes a little easier in terms of planning the content by selecting those topics which the trainee needs. In many cases, however, the one-to-one trainer has to make his or her own list of topics, prepare exercises and practice sessions, etc, as part of the preparation. When this is the case, as it so often is, there are a number of techniques that can be used to determine, select and place in sequence what has to be learned. These include the use of check-lists, interpersonal skills lists, 'family trees' of tasks and procedural guides.

In order to ensure that nothing is left out, the trainer will have to employ basic analytical skills. By observing others doing the job, the trainer is able to take an objective view of what is happening without the distractions of being directly involved. When it is not possible to watch others, trainers can reflect on how they perform the jobs themselves and make notes on each stage and on critical points affecting the job.

To ensure that the content is complete, it is useful to talk through the notes with other trainers and experienced job holders. These techniques and basic analytical methods are equally useful whether we are looking at manual, procedural or social skills.

Check-lists

The check-list is basically a list of what has to be taught, but there is more to it than that. The starting point for most check-lists is a listing of the tasks and sub-tasks carried out by the job holder and arranged in the sequence in which they are performed. There is nothing wrong with this, but there are many examples where the sequence in which the task is performed is not the best sequence for learning it. For example, the day's work for an accounts clerk may begin by checking a computer printout of all of the different types of transaction which had been dealt with on the previous day. The work may then continue with such activities as:

> receiving payments;
> transferring payments to different accounts;
> updating balances;
> closing accounts;
> opening accounts;
> transferring accounts; etc.

It is quite likely that the trainee would gain very little benefit and might even be totally confused if he or she were taught how to check the computer printout without first learning about the different transactions that make up the printout and the procedures for carrying them out.

The start point, then, for the one-to-one trainer is to list the activities that make up the task and then arrange them in the best sequence for learning. Even though the trainee may be able to undertake some of these activities already, they should still be included in correct sequence and confirmed by the trainer as the trainee progresses. There is always more to learn about a job than just being able to perform a number of tasks. It is often the sort of information that the experienced job holder doesn't immediately think about including in training such as 'the reason why' something is done in a particular way, the consequences of error, etc. The way to approach this is to ask about each activity, 'What else do they need in order to do this properly?'. For example:

Preparing Cabbage for Cooking

Shred the leaves using hands: This means that the breaks in the leaf follow natural weaknesses in the leaf formation, so that fewer cells are damaged resulting in minimal vitamin loss.

The amount of detail that has to be gone into in preparing check-lists depends on the nature and complexity of the job. For example, a job involving the use of heavy manual skills such as those used in the building trade would make it difficult and inappropriate to carry around complex check-lists. Also, many building techniques which are taught on-the-job have to be learned when opportunities arise. However, this does not mean that training should not be planned in an appropriate sequence. In more complex and in procedural tasks, detailed check-lists are of clear value especially when some tasks may not be performed frequently. Figure 3.3 is an example of a basic check-list and Figure 3.4 shows how one part can be enlarged, should it be necessary, to include more detail.

Obviously, the amount of detail included in the check-list depends on the competence and confidence of the trainer and on the circumstances in which the training is carried out.

Should it be needed, the check-list in Figure 3.4 could be broken down further to the point where each part becomes a session or lesson in its own right. The amount of detail covered depends very much on the 'need to know'. Lesson or session plans will be discussed in Chapter 4.

Les Davies   Maintenance Department

Concreting

1.   Foundations and Formwork

2.   Different mixes: Sand Cement Aggregate Water

3.   Mixing: by hand
                         using concrete mixer

4.   Tools: Straight edge
                         Spirit level
                         Tamping beam
                         Floats

5.   Finishes: Tamping beam
                         Floats
                         Brush

6.   Protection of new contrete

7.   Storing materials.

8.   Cleaning tools and equipment.

Figure 3.3 *Example of basic check-list*

2.   Different Mixes

        o Cement

- Ordinary (Portland)
- Rapid hardening
- Inhibiting agents
- Pigments

        o Water

- Binding effect on cement
- Effects of too much water
- Effects of impurities

        o Aggregate

- Crushed stone   )
- Uncrushed river gravel   ) strengths
- Mixed crushed/uncrushed)

        o Proportion for

- Foundations, Driveways,
- Heavy duty work
- Paths and thin sections
- Paving, bedding mortar

Etc.

Figure 3.4   *Example of check-list enlarged from Figure 3.3*

'Family trees'

Check-lists are a useful guide for the trainer when the activities that make up the job follow in a set sequence. However, many jobs are more complex and there may not be a specific starting point. For example, a gardener's job will vary with the seasons and with specialized features of the gardens such as roses, water gardens, etc. The job of a customer services officer in a store will vary depending on the nature of the service that the customer wants to obtain, eg, credit facilities, to complain, to exchange goods, etc. In circumstances such as these a number of check-lists may be needed. When this is the case the trainer may need to take an overview of the job in order to place the different tasks into perspective and to provide a context for the trainee who might not be able to see the tasks in relationship to one another. The 'family tree' or job hierarchy can help both trainer and trainee in this respect. Figure 3.5 illustrates how a job can be analysed and set out as a family tree.

Procedural guides

When the job involves decision-making which could result in any of a number of options being taken, the procedural guide is useful not only to analyse what has to be learned but subsequently to serve as a job aid for the trainee on completion of training. Figure 3.6 is an example of this form of guide. There can be any number of guides such as this for a particular job. For example, using the task illustrated in Figure 3.6, there would be a procedure to deal with the candidate allocated a provisional number and who subsequently submits the correct fee.

Interpersonal skills lists

Those who work in the service industries or who have jobs which involve customer contact make considerable use of interpersonal skills. It is often difficult for the trainer to know where to begin when training others. Setting an example by demonstrating the appropriate behaviours is probably the most effective and the most used method, but it helps if the trainer is able to analyse the actual interpersonal skills that they use. One way of doing this is to observe a colleague and note in separate columns what the job holder and the customer or client say and do. The actual lists obviously will vary depending on the situation, the needs of the customer and whether there is any existing relationship between the two. However, as an example, the lists in Figure 3.7 might be representative of a brief interaction between an assistant in a travel agency and a potential customer:

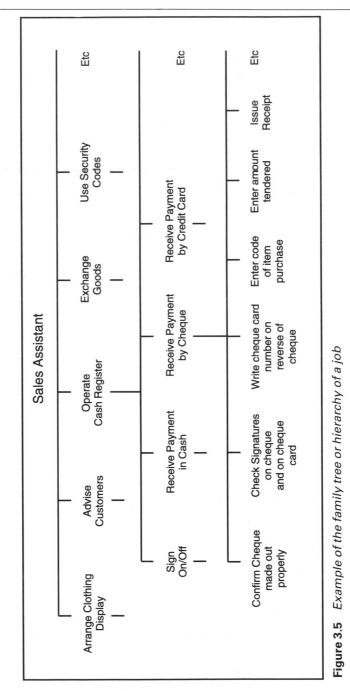

Figure 3.5 *Example of the family tree or hierarchy of a job*

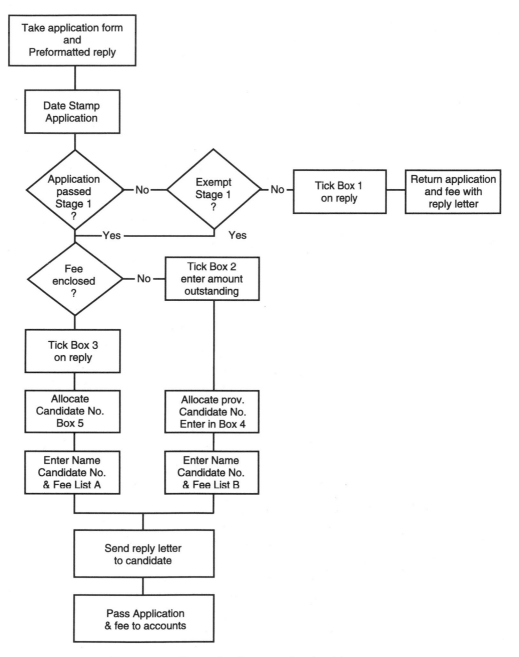

Figure 3.6 *Example of a procedural guide*

65

Assistant	Customer
Greeting/Welcoming	
Giving information	Seeking information
Answering questions	Asking questions
Clarifying	Seeking clarification
Offering alternatives	Stating needs
Explaining	Raising objections
Agreeing/Correcting/ Interrupting	Summarizing information received
Supporting	Confirming needs met
Seeking information	Giving information
Proposing sale	Accepting
Pleasantries	Pleasantries

Figure 3.7 *Example of interpersonal skills lists*

From listings such as these, it is easier for the trainer to establish what the content of training should be. For example 'giving information' in this context suggests product knowledge and, 'explaining' demands good communication skills including listening.

From the check-lists, 'family trees' and procedural guides, it can be appreciated that deciding what trainees have to learn can often be time-consuming and sometimes a little complex but not only is this time well spent, it is most important if training is to be successful.

It is obviously the responsibility of the trainer to ensure that trainees learn and, while this seems to be too obvious a statement to be worthy of mention, there are trainers who demonstrate and explain what to do but who don't actually check to see that trainees have learned. Therefore, it is important to work out, at this preparation stage, how the trainee will demonstrate that they have learned to do everything they need to do and that they know everything that they should know. The best way of doing this is by using a behavioural word or verb at the beginning of each item in the check-lists which indicate how the trainee can be tested. When the trainee has to *do* something this is fairly clear; for example:

Mix concrete by hand.
Operate a cash register.
Issue a receipt.
Allocate a candidate number.
Welcome a customer.
Give information to a customer.

With all of these activities the trainer can observe to see if the trainee performs correctly. However, with most activities the trainee needs a knowledge base to draw upon and before being allowed to perform the task the trainer needs to check that the knowledge base is sound. Therefore, before allowing a trainee to *mix concrete* the trainer would need to confirm that the trainee knows what proportions of sand, cement and aggregate to use and might do this by asking the trainee to *list* the materials and their proportions. Similar questions could be asked to test the knowledge underlying other activities shown above such as:

State the effects of too much water on a mix of concrete.
List the pigments that can be used to colour concrete.
State the fee payable for part 2 of the exam.

Most of the statements relating to demonstrating knowledge begin with 'state', 'list', 'describe', 'explain' etc.

Many readers will recognize these statements as the 'performance' elements of training objectives. Those who have the support of training departments are likely to have the training objectives prepared for them. When this is the case they are likely to be given other vital information at the same time. That information should include details of the 'standard' that the trainees are expected to reach by the end of training and a listing of the equipment, materials, environmental factors, etc, needed to perform each task – these are referred to as the 'conditions'. The following are examples of objectives as they might be set out in a training document.

Example 1

Performance	Conditions	Standard
Mix concrete by hand.	Given: Cement, Aggregate, Sand, Water Supply, Shovel.	Correct proportions of materials. Consistency to satisfaction of trainer.

Example 2

Performance	Conditions	Standard
Process an application for an examination.	Given: Application Form and Fee, Pre-formatted reply, Stationery items.	Correctly – to the satisfaction of the trainer.

For those trainers who are not lucky enough to have training objectives prepared for them, it can be seen that task lists and family tree analyses, etc, can be developed into this format. The advantages are that the trainer can see quite clearly what the trainee has to do, what equipment and materials are needed, and how to confirm that the trainee has learned. In a large number of instances in one-to-one training the standard is likely to be 'to the satisfaction of the trainer' but it is a useful exercise for trainers to work out what will 'satisfy' them.

Where will the Training Take Place?

The relative advantages and disadvantages of on-the-job and off-the-job training have been discussed already. At this stage of preparing to train, '*where*' should be regarded in terms of the total environment; that is, not only the location but the equipment and materials that are available in that location.

In off-the-job training situations there may be a 'quiet room' available or it may be a case of having to use someone's office when they are out. Establishing where training will take place must be confirmed as soon as possible and if there is a booking system for the use of training rooms or offices, the trainer must ensure that they book the room and have all of the relevant equipment and materials *in situ* when training begins. The authors recall the circumstances of a trainer who, in her turn, had to train in the committee room in a cricket club which was located some eight miles from the work location. Great care had to be taken to ensure that all of the materials that she needed were taken with her. In addition to collecting large numbers of documents and forms it may be necessary to prepare specimen or case-study material when there is no 'live' work for the trainee to practise with.

When training takes place in the job location, there is a far greater probability that everything in the way of material and resources will be to hand, but there is no guarantee. The trainer should again prepare a detailed list of all that is required and ensure that it is available when training begins.

When training takes place in a noisy environment or one with constant customer contact, it is useful to find a quiet space somewhere nearby so that the trainee can be taken to one side when detailed or complex matters have to be explained or so that feedback can be given. However, when this is done, the trainee has to be re-introduced to the real work environment at appropriate stages in order to ensure that what has been learned can be applied properly in real situations.

In terms of the physical nature of the environment, the trainer should not take anything for granted. Being offered the use of a room does not necessarily mean that there will be a table in it or if there is now, there may not be when the first training session begins. The fact that there is a power point which might be needed for a calculator does not necessarily mean that it works. Detailed preparation of the environment will need to be undertaken immediately before training begins and this will be discussed in Chapter 4.

When will the Training Take Place?

The word *when* refers to all time factors concerning training. First, there is the need to know when the training will begin and second, to clarify the period over which training will take place.

The start time for training needs to be established because it has been seen already that a considerable amount of preparation has to be done before training begins. When trainers are experienced, the lead time that is needed for preparation is not very long and they are able to take on a trainee at very short notice because their preparation has been done for previous trainees and needs only to be updated. However, for those who have not trained anyone before, there is a very definite need for realistic preparation time as well as training for themselves in one-to-one training skills if they have not received it already. Only then does the training stand a chance of being successful. In some cases trainers may need to be a little bold and emphasize this to sponsors; not everyone appreciates what is involved.

The period of time over which training will take place is also important for planning. The first consideration usually has to be, 'will it be long enough?'. The pressures on line managers and supervisors to have staff up and running is often reflected in the short amount of time that they are prepared to allocate to training. The trainer is always likely to have to negotiate for more time and should be prepared to present a list of topics or the training objectives to sponsors and ask them to prioritize what they would like to have trained. Unhelpful responses such as 'all of it', or flattering responses such as 'I know that if anyone can do it, you can', should be responded to with a realistic assessment of precisely what can be achieved in the time so that there will not be any unrealistic expectations on the part of the trainee, the trainer or the sponsor.

Another aspect of time that needs to be thought about is how the training time will be allocated. It might be that a block of a week or a specific number of days is allocated to training, or the time may be broken up into sessions of one day per week, two hours a day, every afternoon for three weeks, etc.

The trainer needs to take careful note of such time allocations. When training is continuous and intensive, the trainee could become saturated very quickly, especially if he or she falls into the 'older worker' category. On the other hand, there may be certain tasks for which the trainee needs 'hands on' experience, and such opportunities may arise only on certain days or only in the mornings, etc. Therefore, timing needs to be matched very carefully with learning opportunities.

How the Training will be Done

At the beginning of this chapter it was explained that in order to prepare thoroughly the trainer needs to think about *who* has to trained, *why* they need to be trained, *what* they need to be trained in and *where* and *when* the training would take place. This information, together with an understanding of the ways in which people learn as described in Chapter 2, should put the trainer in a position where he or she can decide how the training can be carried out most effectively. The model for one-to-one training which was introduced in Chapter 1 is sufficiently flexible to be used as a structure for most individual sessions within the overall training plan. Its application is discussed in detail in Chapter 4; coaching is discussed in Chapter 5.

4 One-to-one Training

> SUMMARY <

In this chapter you will learn about:
- The application of a model for one-to-one training.
- The skills, strategies and tactics used by one-to-one trainers to teach manual, procedural and social skills.

At the end of the first chapter a model for one-to-one training was introduced (see Figure 1.3). Chapters 2 and 3 described the extent and depth of preparation needed before training should begin and the factors that affect how and why people learn. In this chapter the model is reintroduced and stage by stage it is shown how the trainer can draw upon the preparation that has been undertaken and a knowledge of motivation and learning to apply a number of techniques and skills which will lead to effective training.

Preparation

It might be thought that sufficient preparation had been done already and readers understandably might ask if they are to spend all of their time preparing without actually getting to train anyone. However, the nature of the preparation described here is that which takes place immediately before a training session and ensures that none of the

71

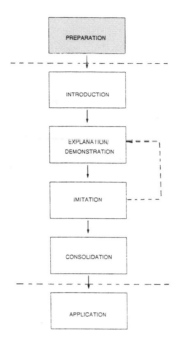

longer-term preparation is wasted or spoiled by a failure to pay attention to detail at the moment when it counts. The kind of preparation referred to here relates to materials, equipment, environment, the trainee, the trainer, and supervisors and other staff.

Materials

The materials for any particular session obviously vary depending upon the task being taught. Builders will need to think in terms of quantities of sand and cement, caterers in terms of ingredients for cooking, clerical staff will have to consider forms and stationery, etc. The questions listed below are not exhaustive but serve as a guide to prepare a check-list which should be included in the trainer's notes.

— Are there sufficient materials for demonstration and practice?
— Are there sufficient materials if the trainee needs more practice than usual?
— Are the materials arranged in the order in which they will be used?

- Are the materials for the next session easily accessible in case the trainee learns quickly?
- Are all tools and equipment to hand?
- Are all forms and stationery up to date and in current use?
- Are all reference books, documents, job guides, etc, to hand if needed?
- Are references in manuals, etc, marked for easy access?
- Are there examples of completed work available to show the trainee what is being aimed at?
- Are notes or handouts available for the trainee?
- Are visual aids to hand?
- Are tutor notes to hand?

Equipment

It is not always possible for trainers to have control over or possession of equipment in the same way as they might by keeping their own stock of forms or small items of equipment such as calculators or their own tools. Even when training takes place in the trainer's own work station there are a number of checks that are important to carry out. The credibility of the trainer can be dented if equipment is found not to work or fails. The following are worth thinking about:

- Is there sufficient fuel to run mechanical equipment?
- Is there an electrical power source for equipment and can cables reach? Is an extension cable needed?
- Has the equipment been tested and are all functions working properly?
- Are there any faults or is there damage to the equipment that breach safety regulations?
- Are there any parts of the equipment that are likely to fail as a result of normal usage? Are spares to hand?
- Is safety clothing needed and available for the trainee, eg, gloves, helmets, etc?
- If computers or computerized equipment is being used, have the correct programs been loaded?

Environment

Most people who have built up experience in a particular job, rightly or wrongly, develop short cuts which become local custom and practice. This includes how they organize their working environment. Trainers are no exception to this. However, in training there is a need to pay attention to the environment on two counts; first, to ensure that there are no distractions or lack of space to work and second, to influence the trainee to develop 'good habits' in the way that they approach their work. No trainer should ever be in a position where materials and documents have to be swept into a confused heap to find space for training. The following factors should be taken into consideration:

- Is the working environment clean (within the limitations of the nature of the task)?
- Has all waste material been disposed of?
- Has all unwanted current work been put on one side?
- Are the levels of heating, lighting and ventilation sufficient?
- Have any instances of bad practice, poor workmanship or general slackness been removed? (Eg, last year's calendar hanging in an infrequently used work space does not create the best of impressions).
- Is there a chair available for the trainee, if needed?
- Are all training materials, tools, etc, set out in the order in which they will be used and have all distractions been removed?
- Do telephone calls need to be diverted to avoid interruptions?
- Is there a need to put a warning notice on the training room door?
- Is there a 'quiet area' available so that aspects of the task can be explained away from the noise of the work environment?
- Have all safety factors been observed?

Trainee

When trainees begin training they should have been well-prepared in the longer-term by pre-training briefings conducted by their line managers or supervisors and possibly by their trainers as well. At this stage the preparation immediately before training begins is concerned with comfort and readiness of the trainee. Depending on how the training has been structured, trainees may have been fully employed on other tasks only minutes before a training session begins, others may have had to travel to the trainer's work location and arrive after a hurried journey. This is not a criticism of work planning but a realistic appraisal of how organizations have to operate in order to make the best use of resources. To ensure that the trainee is ready, it is useful to ask about the following:

- Has the trainee just come from a busy and demanding environment?
- Has the trainee been under stress or encountered any problems in work before this training session which still cause concern?

— Has the trainee had to travel to attend this session and if so, what was the journey like?
— Has the trainee had a break before beginning training?
— When has the next break been planned?
— Is the trainee hot, cold, out of breath from travelling?
— Does the trainee need to use the men's or ladies' room? Does he or she know where these facilities are?

Trainer

It is just as important for the trainer to be ready to run a training session as it is for the trainee to be ready to receive it. When the trainer is also involved in day-to-day operational work, having to fit in a training session for someone else is often felt to be an interruption, if not an imposition. The result can be hasty and incomplete training, lack of attention to the trainee's needs and impatience and anger if the trainee is slow to learn. If training sessions have been planned properly and there is a departmental commitment to training, then fitting in the sessions should not create a big problem. However, the readiness of the trainer is a key factor and all trainers need to consider their readiness by going through a mental check-list to consider factors such as the following:

— Have I reached a point in my own work where I can now run a training session without worrying about something that is outstanding?
— Do I feel enthusiastic about the training or do I need to have a short break, calm down, get my breath back, have a drink, etc?
— Would it help if I freshened up a bit?
— Do I look neat and tidy or am I dressed properly and do I look like the experienced worker that I should be?
— Have I been eating something which has made my breath smell and could make learning uncomfortable?

Supervisors and Other Workers

Interruptions are probably the biggest nuisance in any form of training and this is particularly the case with one-to-one training. On-the-job training has the outward appearance of being less formal than off-job-training or training which takes place away from the work location. Whereas people are hesitant to walk into a classroom to interrupt, they do not have the same reluctance when it comes to interrupting a one-to-one session. Interruptions of either a social or a work-based nature which could wait can become quite a common occurrence. This becomes even more noticeable when it is the supervisor who is conducting the training and someone needs help or a decision to be made. The trainer can reduce the number of interruptions by considering the following:

- Has everyone been told that I am running a training session?
- Do they know when I shall be available before and after the session?
- Have I made clear the circumstances in which it is appropriate to interrupt?
- Does everyone know the importance of the training session?
- Are people appreciative of the complexity of the material/skills that has to be learned?

Introduction

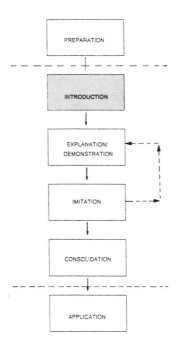

When all of the long-term and immediate preparation has been undertaken the training can actually begin. The broken line in the diagram of the model indicates that preparation is a pre-training activity.

Briefings will have gone some way towards introducing the training as a whole; however, this is not sufficient. The programme of training and each individual session needs to be introduced properly. Trainers who have not been trained are quite likely to leap into delivering the technical content of training without introducing their material. They probably feel more secure on familiar ground. However, those trainers who have been trained will testify to the benefits felt by themselves and by their trainees when well-structured introductions are used. The introduction does not take up a great amount of time but the investment in a few minutes is well worthwhile.

There is no prescribed structure or set sequence to follow in the introduction. What goes into the introduction will depend on what has to be taught, what was learned in a previous session, the trainee's progress to date, etc. If the session that the trainer has to deliver is the first in the training programme, then there will be a need to introduce the programme and then the first session.

Trainers 'get a feel' for the way in which they want to sequence their introductions just as they do for the way in which they sequence the subject matter of the session. The important thing is that an introduction should flow in a logical and coherent fashion rather than being a series of disjointed points. Carefully prepared introductions can have very positive effects on the motivation of the trainee.

The headings listed below should be regarded as a menu from which those that are relevant can be selected and sequenced to suit the trainer.

Headings to Introduce the Training Programme

● Establish or maintain rapport

A good working relationship is essential for successful training. This is appreciated by those trainers who teach groups but in one-to-one situations it is even more important. One-to-one training involves continuous direct contact between trainer and trainee. It is important to begin by using a few minutes chatting about common interests or matters of general interest so that both parties can get to know one another a little better. If they have met before or been involved together in training before it is still of value to maintain the rapport by having a short chat. Both parties are then likely to feel more relaxed and ready to work. However, a word of warning – don't get so engrossed in matters of mutual interest that the training is neglected.

●**Find out if the trainee is left- or right-handed**

This may seem very trivial but when hands have to be used to perform the task, even if it is writing, the trainer needs to be sitting where the trainee can be seen. Similarly, the trainee needs to be able to see demonstrations clearly.

● **Outline the structure of the training programme**

Most of us prefer to know what we are 'letting ourselves in for'. That is, we like to know what we are going to be taught and the demands that are going to be made of us. It helps to focus the mind and to pace ourselves when we see the complete picture. 'Family trees' and procedural charts can be put to good use here by showing the trainee the scope of the work.

● **Confirm details of pre-training briefing**

Although the trainer may have gone to great pains to ensure that a proper briefing has been given by a line manager or supervisor, experience has shown that on many occasions this does not happen. The trainer needs to ensure that the briefing received by the trainee is accurate. When it is not, the trainer needs to clarify matters and subsequently to nudge the supervisor to make amends before training has gone too far.

● **Confirm trainee's level of knowledge, skill and experience**

During the preparation stage, the trainer should have gathered information about the existing levels of knowledge, skill and experience of the trainee. This needs to be confirmed. It is possible that some learning has taken place since the initial preparation was done. It is also possible that the information given to the trainer was not accurate. The authors have experienced those who 'only need to brush up' on a few points but who in reality know little or nothing. The converse has also been experienced.

● **Establish own credibility**

Trainees like to feel confident that what they are being trained to do is accurate and is good practice. It is worthwhile, without it sounding boastful, for the trainer to explain their own level of involvement, experience and qualifications in the tasks that are being trained. Not only does it establish credibility but it shows the trainee what expertise there is to draw upon when it comes to asking questions or asking for advice.

- **Clarify procedures for testing and reporting**

While a number of organizations avoid formal testing and reporting, there is a growing lobby for feedback to be given. Line managers need to know what tasks they can give an individual and be confident that they can do it after their training. Similarly, trainees who have done well like it to be recognized, and those who need further support after training want to feel confident that they will not be given tasks that they will not be able to perform. It is helpful to show a trainee a copy of a report form that may be used and to outline the nature of any tests.

- **Administrative points**

There are usually administrative points that need to be included with all forms of training. The amount of information that has to be given will depend on the trainee's familiarity with the environment. Information may need to be given on toilet facilities, accommodation, travel, first aid, security, fire regulations, etc.

- **Any questions**

Opportunity should be given to the trainee to ask any relevant questions. However succinct our explanations may be, there is often a need to have points clarified. It is at this point that those who enter the programme with negative attitudes question why they have to do the training or claim that they do not need it; this might also come to light when the briefing is discussed. Trainers need to be on their guard here and not try to play the line manager. It is better to refer back to the line manager straight away rather than embark on a fruitless task.

Headings to Introduce a Training Session

- **Revision/review**

When training sessions have been separated by a break for coffee or lunch, the trainer needs to refocus the trainee by revising or reviewing what was learned in the previous session. This might consist of a summary of what was covered, the key points that were learned, weaknesses that needed to be worked on and, possibly, questioning or further practice on areas which were not quite up to standard.

- **Topic**

This is a brief explanation of what the session will concentrate on so that the trainee can begin to focus attention on the new topic.

- **Confirm trainee's level of knowledge or skill**

When trainees have had some exposure to, or experience of, a job before they begin training, they are likely to have developed some knowledge or skill already. Rather than making training tedious by teaching them what they already know or accepting at face value that they have the knowledge that they claim to have, the trainer should question the trainee to confirm the level he or she has reached. When trainees claim to know the subject matter of the session completely, the trainer should test them by using the questions and exercises that have been prepared for the end of the session. If they are successful, they can be congratulated and the next topic can be introduced. If they fail, they can be shown their errors so that they appreciate the need for training and the session can continue.

- **Context**

Not every session that is taught follows on naturally from the previous one and sometimes it is difficult to see how the session fits into the overall pattern of the job. The trainee needs to have the topic which has to be studied placed in context by relating it to what has gone before, what follows and any other associated or linked tasks. This helps to show the relevance of the session.

- **Objectives**

Objectives were discussed in Chapter 3. Both trainer and trainee need to be very clear about what the outcomes of the session will be. The trainer needs to explain very clearly and precisely what the trainee will have to do to demonstrate that they have learned, for example:

1. List the safety precautions that need to be taken when using electrical equipment.
2. Operate an electric band saw.

- **Motivation**

The relevance of the subject matter to the trainee's job is usually sufficient to motivate; however, there are occasions when this might not be sufficient. The objectives state what the trainee will be able to do but there is a need to show why they should bother to learn it.

Motivational factors might include satisfaction in doing the job well, having a skill that can be used in other contexts, work will be easier or done more quickly, the appreciation that will be shown by co-workers or customers, etc. There are occasions when the subject matter and the job are boring and dull. In fact, it may be part of a job that no one likes to do. There is little point in the trainer trying to convince the trainee that it is the most exciting task that they could be called upon to do. The trainer's credibility will be seriously at stake if this happens. In these circumstances it is better to be honest and tell them that the task is tedious. However, at the same time, they need to be told why the task has to be done and what the consequences might be if it is not done properly. If attention is likely to wander while a job holder is involved with boring tasks more errors are likely to occur. Trainees need to appreciate the fact that all jobs have boring elements and if they are aware of them they will know when they have to apply themselves with a little more vigour.

- **Structure and Timing**

This explains to the trainee how the session will be presented and how much time will be spent on different aspects of the training. Included here would be: what the trainer will do, explain and demonstrate, what the trainee will be expected to do, details of testing or assessment, etc. When people know what is expected of them in terms of observing, taking in information, practising and being tested, etc, they are able to prepare themselves psychologically and feel more comfortable with the session. If there is a difficult test that they have to do at the end of the session, they may not like the idea, but nevertheless feel more comfortable in knowing what lies ahead.

- **Ground rules**

When the task being taught involves the observation of safety rules and procedures, these need to be emphasized to the trainee at the outset. Other 'ground rules' might include telling the trainee that they can ask questions at any time or that there will be an opportunity to ask questions at stages during the session, etc.

- **Jargon and technical language**

All jobs develop their own jargon or technical language. It becomes so much a part of daily usage that sometimes the trainee's needs are overlooked. They fear asking what it means because the very fact that the trainer uses various terms and phrases frequently tends to suggest that the trainee ought to understand. Apart from emphasizing that the trainee should ask about any such terms that they are not familiar with, the trainer can list in the introduction any new terms and technical language that will be met.

- ● **Showing a finished article**

When it is appropriate, the trainer can show a completed item which shows the trainee what they will be expected to produce at the end of the session or the programme. For example, a chef may find it useful to show a trainee a cake, which has been decorated for a wedding, as a standard for them to aim for.

It was stated earlier that the headings for the introduction should be regarded as a menu from which the trainer chooses and arranges in an order which suits their own style. The examples below give an idea of how this might be done.

Example 1

> Before lunch we looked at the procedure for receiving payments from customers by post and you processed a few of these by yourself. The one thing that you needed to be reminded about was that you should complete the discount eligibility box when payment has been made within seven days – this means that the customer will be eligible for discount on the next order.
>
> Now we are going to learn how to deal with underpayments and overpayments – that is, when the customer sends too much or too little money. So, by the end of this session you will be able to complete the appropriate pre-formatted letters and annotate the customer's account. It is important to get this right because otherwise we could get involved in lengthy time-wasting correspondence and no one will thank us for that.
>
> We shall be using two pre-formatted letters and four fields on the customer account screen on your VDU.
>
> Because we do not get many over- or under-payments, I have prepared some specimens for us to practise on and I have set aside two from today's work for you to do for real. Don't forget, ask questions whenever you like.

This introduction would take no more than two minutes and yet it sets the scene and leaves the trainee in no doubt about what is going to be done, how and why. It is also worth noting that in this example the word 'we' has been used; this helps to show that the learning experience is one that is shared by both trainer and trainee.

Example 2

The lawn that you are looking at I finished cutting a couple of hours ago. But to get it looking as good as this needs more attention than just cutting it. It needs to be fed, treated for weeds, raked, spiked and so on. At the moment the grass is growing quickly and so we shall concentrate on cutting to begin with. I will teach you the other things at different times in the season.

To cut it so that it has the nice, straight stripes that you can see, you need to do more than walk in a straight line. You need to be able to maintain the mower properly and that includes adjusting the height of the cut. That's what I'm going to teach you now and then you'll have visitors to the park admiring your handiwork. I'll show you how it's done and then you can have a go. You'll be able to cut a stretch of grass at different heights of cut so that you can see the difference. After that I'll teach you how to clean and maintain the mower.

Explanation, Demonstration, Imitation

The stages of explanation, demonstration and imitation cannot be separated as easily as the other stages because in most cases they are concurrent activities. There are occasions when demonstrations of critical aspects of a task are done in silence and prefaced or followed by an explanation, but for the most part we explain as we demonstrate.

The way in which the trainer applies different techniques and learning strategies is likely to vary depending on whether the task being taught is associated with manual, procedural or social skills. Some techniques and strategies are common to all three types of skill, others are more specific to particular skills.

There are two models or sequences of activity which provide useful guidelines for the explanation – demonstration – imitation stage.

Sequence A

1. Trainer demonstrates at normal speed.
2. Trainer demonstrates and explains at slow speed.
3. Trainer and trainee perform activity together.
4. Trainee performs activity alone (and explains what he or she is doing).

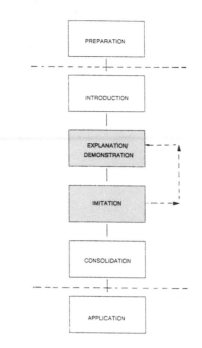

This model can be adapted to suit the needs of the task and the ability or aptitude of the trainee. For example, the model as it stands would probably be ideal for teaching someone to knit or to learn other skills which require manual dexterity, but if someone were being taught to fill in a form, stages 2 and 4 would be a more appropriate application. In teaching someone how to interview, provided that suitable explanation is given before and after the event, stages 1 and 4 would be most appropriate.

Sequence B

1. Trainer demonstrates and explains.
2. Trainer demonstrates again while trainee explains what is being done.
3. Trainee performs task and explains what he or she is doing.
4. Trainee performs task.

This kind of sequence can also be varied in the way that it is used but the format presented here has been found appropriate for teaching procedures with the visual display unit of a computer.

General Features of a Good Explanation

Confusion is caused by garbled, unprepared explanations. Even though trainers know their job very thoroughly, explaining it to someone else is not as easy as it might be. You only have to look at the explanations or directions on food packages to see how easy it is to come to grief if the directions are followed without reading them fully and organizing the sequence in your mind. For example:

> Place the can in a saucepan of boiling water for fifteen minutes, remove carefully, open the can and serve. It is important to punch two holes in the top of the can before immersing it in the boiling water.

A good explanation will be:

- **In a logical sequence**

Actions need to be explained in the sequence in which they occur. When there is an option of taking one of a number alternatives at a decision point, it may be seful to use a visual aid such as a flow chart or algorithm to keep the trainee focused.

- **Clear and concise**

There is no need to 'over explain'; the more words that are used, the more the trainee has to remember or to filter out. Simple instructions are usually sufficient; however, there should not be an economy on words when there is a need to explain the reason why. For example, the instruction 'Punch two holes in the top of the can before immersing it in the boiling water' becomes more meaningful when it is explained that 'otherwise it could explode and cause serious injury'. Far too often the 'reason why' is missing from explanations.

- **Relevant**

Trainers who are enthusiastic or those who are disorganized tend to stray into other areas which do not have relevance to the task in hand.

- **Accurate**

This ought to be an obvious feature of an explanation; however, trainers may have developed their own custom and practice or their own shortcuts which could be passed on to the trainee who might subsequently be taken to task by their supervisor.

- **In digestible chunks**

No one can assimilate information if they are given too much at one time. Time is needed to receive, absorb and mentally organize one chunk of information before going on to the next.

- **Delivered at an appropriate speed and with interest**

The key guideline here is for the trainer to sound interested and interesting. If the trainer is interested in both the subject matter and in the trainee, then the trainee is more likely to develop an enthusiasm for the training.

A good explanation will avoid:

- **Jargon**

Although jargon or technical language is needed if the trainee is to fit into the environment, it needs to be used sparingly early in training and clarified when it is used.

- **Assumptions**

An appreciation of the trainee's existing level of knowledge should have been gained during preparation or at the beginning of the session, but it is always worth checking that they understand and it is better to err on the side of some repetition than having a bewildered or confused trainee.

- **Ambiguity**

What makes sense to us as experienced workers may not to an inexperienced trainee. Care must be taken to ensure that there is no doubt in the trainee's mind about what has been explained.

A good explanation will include:

- **Asking questions**

This is particularly the case when explanations may be lengthy and the trainer needs to confirm understanding at different stages.

- **Use of visual aids**

It is often thought that visual aids are used only when groups are being taught. The block of writing paper on a table serves the same purpose for the one-to-one trainer as the flip chart does for those who teach groups. A simple diagram can help to make an explanation much clearer.

- **Looking at the trainee**

It is difficult to pick up many of the non-verbal cues of a trainee when sitting alongside them. The trainer needs to make a conscious effort to turn and look at them; cues such as nodding or looking puzzled soon tell us whether or not the explanation is good enough.

General Features of a Good Demonstration

There is more to a demonstration than just having a trainee watch an experienced worker or a trainer perform a job or task. Those of us who may have watched an experienced decorator paper a ceiling and then tried to imitate will probably confirm that something in the way of a proper demonstration is needed if we are to stand any chance of being successful.

A good demonstration will be:

- **Visible**

In a number of tasks our bodies or hands are likely to obscure the vision of the trainee. The trainee must be placed on the side of the trainer where vision is not impeded. Sometimes it may be necessary to stand back from the task or to exaggerate movements to show the correct way to do something.

- **In stages**

Apart from those tasks which are of such complexity that a number of actions have to take place simultaneously, it is easier to understand if the demonstration is given stage by stage. It might also be linked with practising stage by stage. This would be very appropriate when part learning is involved.

- **Used in conjunction with real material**

As far as is possible the real equipment and materials should be used unless this is costly or time-consuming. When this is the case a good simulation is needed. For example it would be unrealistic to have a submarine available at all times for electricians to have demonstrated to them how to replace fuses in a fuse box. The fuse box itself or a realistic model of the fuse box would be sufficient.

- **Done at an appropriate speed**

In the same way that demonstrating by stages assists learning, slowing down the speed also assists during the early part of training. Someone who is accomplished at hand knitting or lace making would have to slow down to a speed well below their normal working speed to make the demonstration effective.

- **Accompanied by an explanation**

Apart from intricate movements which need absolute concentration, demonstrations are more effective when accompanied by an explanation. Taking hold of an instrument in a particular way may be very clearly demonstrated but it is more meaningful when an explanation of why is given.

Explaining and Demonstrating Manual Tasks

Some features of explanations and demonstrations are more specifically applicable to learning manual skills. These include the use of the senses, rhythms, guidance, work pieces and examples, and part and whole learning. Manual skills range from what might be described as heavy work such as is found in the building and transport industries to those which require a high level of manual dexterity such as using a keyboard or making jewellery.

The *senses* can be used to help the trainee to experience the standard that they have to achieve. At different stages in the process the trainer can break off to allow the trainee to experience such things as:

- the smoothness of a piece of timber which is being planed;
- the taste of a sauce as different ingredients are added;
- the sound of a petrol engine which is being tuned;
- the consistency of mortar being mixed for building;
- the resistance of a moving part in a machine which is being serviced;
- the weight of a tool or a piece of equipment;
- the temperature of water for bathing a baby;
- the accuracy of measurement using a spirit level, etc.

Many manual skills, particularly those which involve a repetitive element, seem to develop a form of *rhythm*. This rhythm is brought about by slight pauses in the cycle or process. A rhythm which becomes very obvious to us when repairs or refurbishing is being carried out is that which is hammered out by the carpenter knocking in nails; for each nail there is a particular rhythm of hammer blows which often ends with two sharp taps to confirm that the nail is firmly in place. Winfield (1988) sees these rhythms as a form of metronome which the brain has developed in order to organize the task and he gives a number of examples from every-day activities:

- a bricklayer pauses after laying a brick before scooping up fresh mortar on the trowel;
- a painter pauses for a moment after loading a brush with paint;
- a kitchen hand punctuates the task of peeling potatoes by dipping the potato into the water to clean off the scrapings.

The same rhythmical patterns can be observed in gardeners digging a vegetable plot and by labourers shovelling sand into barrows.

These rhythms tend to be learned rather than taught and can be easily picked up by the trainee when the trainer adopts the learning model which involves the trainee doing the task with the trainer. That is when imitation and demonstration are almost simultaneous.

Linked closely with the use of senses and developing rhythms is the *guidance* that the trainer can give. In terms of manual skills, guidance is usually physical in some way. For example the trainer can guide a trainee's hand in using a saw so that the trainee can feel or sense the amount of pressure that should be used on the downward cut compared with that needed to draw the saw upwards again. Other examples might include:

- moving a trainee's hand to the different control functions of a tape recorder to pick up the sequence to make a sound recording;
- moving a trainee's hand to guide a float when applying plaster to a wall;
- guiding a trainee's hand to apply a bandage to support an ankle.

Many manual tasks result in some form of end product and it is always useful for a trainee to see what the finished item looks like before beginning to learn how to produce it. The use of *pieces* and *examples* help greatly in this respect. Drawing on the illustration of applying a bandage to support an ankle, it would be useful if the trainee was able to see a bandaged ankle first so that some sense would be seen in the way in which the bandage is applied. In the same way, an electrical plug correctly wired can be shown to the trainee at the outset of the session. When real examples cannot be used, pictures are a good substitute.

The technique of *part* and *whole learning* was described in Chapter 2. In the learning of manual skills this technique comes into its own. By using part learning for lengthy or difficult tasks, the stages of explanation, demonstration and imitation are used a number of times before the task is practised as a whole.

Practising Manual Skills (Imitation)

This stage in the one-to-one training model is not a time when the trainer can switch off and leave the trainee to his or her own devices. It is a time when the trainer needs to be alert and to exercise a wide range of skills. The following are particularly relevant to manual skills:

- **Observing**

to see how well the trainee performs and noting learning points which will need to be discussed when the task has been completed.

- **Analysing**

any errors that are made to see if the cause can be attributed to anything that may have been misunderstood or not seen properly, and to consider how the problem can be put right. For example, a left-handed person may have to hold a tool differently from a right-handed person.

- **Intervening**

when it is necessary, to help the manual process to flow. Interventions can include cueing the trainee when something is about to happen (eg, water is about to boil), prompting or reminding them to do something (eg, stir the paint before using it) or stopping them when danger is imminent (eg, from a power source that has not been isolated) or when they are likely to do something which would mean starting all over again (eg, adding salt instead of sugar to a cake mixture). The opposite of this is to resist intervening when the trainee is about to make an error from which a lesson would be learned. There is nothing wrong with allowing trainees to learn from their mistakes.

- **Encouraging**

with the occasional word of praise or confirmation that the trainee is making satisfactory or good progress is a strong motivator, and spurs the trainee on to greater efforts.

Explanation and Demonstration of Procedural Skills

Procedural tasks make up a large part of many jobs. In a manufacturing and industrial context, procedures are likely to include such activities as inspections, fault finding, maintenance, etc. In administrative and commercial contexts one can readily identify such procedures as form filling, data analysis, data input using a terminal and document checking.

Learning a procedure involves acquiring an understanding of the sequence of steps that make up a particular task together with the knowledge and mental or physical skill associated with each step. These steps take the form of what have come to be described as chains and algorithms.

Chains

A chain is made up of steps which have to be carried out in a fixed order with no permitted deviation from sequence. A simple illustration of this concept is given in Figure 4.1. Other examples might include the sequence of steps in changing gear in a car or changing a wheel.

Depending on the length of the chain and the complexity of the steps which make it up, there are a number of tactics which the trainer can use to teach the procedure. For short, simple chains:

1. Demonstrate or show the trainee the whole procedure; intersperse the demonstration with any appropriate explanation whilst taking care not to overload the trainee with information.
2. Go through the procedure again getting the trainee to talk through or explain what actions are required at each step (if necessary verbally prompt or correct the trainee).
3. Get the trainee to carry out the procedure whilst at the same time requiring him or her to give a commentary on the important features of each step in the procedure. If it is required prompt, guide or correct the trainee.
4. Direct the trainee to repeat the preceding stage just to check full mastery.

For long or complex chains:

1. Either give the trainee a brief overview of the whole procedure, highlighting the main stages, or show the trainee the end product, eg, the completed form or product.
2. Employ the 'progressive parts' method, which would involve distributed practice of more and more steps of the whole task – A; B; A + B; C; A + B + C; D; etc. If the chain is long but each step is relatively simple then a variation of the progressive parts could be used, eg, A + B; C + D; A + B + C + D; etc.

The trainer must ensure that the trainee has the necessary knowledge and skills to carry out each step before attempting to combine steps.

The tactics for short, simple chains could be used when teaching the trainee to combine steps. However, a word of warning: because it could

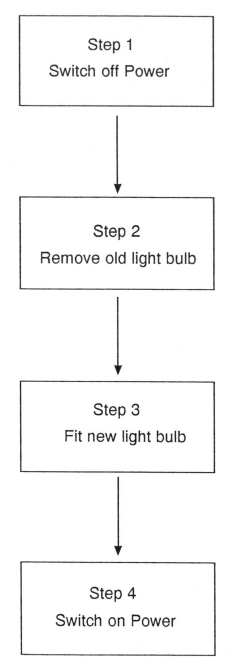

Figure 4.1 *Illustration of a simple chain*

become boring or demotivating, it may not always be sensible to ask the trainee to give a commentary when he or she is demonstrating his or her ability to combine steps.

Some procedural chains are a mixture of simple and complex steps and therefore a combination of the above tactics would have to be employed.

Algorithms and discriminations

An algorithm, as it is used in this context, is made up of a series of steps which include decision points to determine what the next step in the procedure should be. At those decision points the trainee has to discriminate between different sets of conditions in order to select the way forward. Discriminations of this kind may also occur within a step of a simple chain. The basic concept of the algorithm is shown in Figure 4.2. The conditions that the trainee might have to discriminate between could include such factors as:

- ages of applicants for life insurance policies;
- grade of oil used in a particular engine;
- code numbers of spare parts in store;
- qualifications of candidates seeking exemption from examinations or membership of professional organizations.

It can be seen that there are many similarities with the procedural analysis shown in Figure 3.6.

In teaching the trainee to discriminate, the trainer should initially distinguish what is to be discriminated. The trainee should be allowed to discriminate an easy problem or distinction to begin with and then, if necessary, work towards harder or more difficult discriminations. A good deal of practice with difficult examples, spaced out over a number of sessions, would be advantageous.

Algorithms can be taught using similar tactics to those outlined for chains and discriminations. For simple algorithms the whole method would be appropriate. More complex algorithms would probably have to be learned in stages. These stages may be defined by the steps coming before and after the main decision points. It has been suggested that the most appropriate tactic for teaching complex algorithms is for the sections that follow the decision point to be taught separately before illustrating for the trainee how to make the decision or discrimination. The theory is that it will be a lot easier for the trainee to make the distinction once he or she has an understanding of the steps that make up the alternative chains.

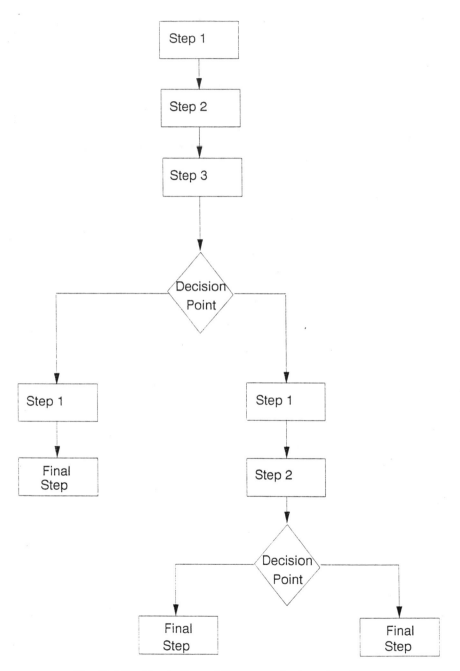

Figure 4.2 *Illustration of the concept of an algorithm*

Learning of Concepts and Principles Related to Procedural Tasks

In the process of learning a procedure the trainee may have to learn new concepts and principles in relation to the whole procedure or to particular steps.

A *concept* is a general idea or notion about a group or class of objects or events and can usually be defined verbally or symbolically, that is, using mathematical notation, or diagrams. Such concepts might include leadership styles, qualities of leadership, management climate, etc. The learning tactics recommended for teaching concepts are:

- Where possible display the idea diagrammatically or in symbolic form.
- Present a range of examples and non-examples of the concept.
- Emphasize the links and relationship between related ideas.
- Ask the trainee to identify the similarities and differences between the new concept and other related ideas.
- Encourage the trainee to think and talk actively about the concept and what it means.

Ideas or concepts are linked together to form a *principle* or *rule of action*. For example, the concepts of percentage, turnover rate, bulk purchase, etc, may all be linked to the principle of discount. The appropriate learning tactics to use to teach principles are as follows:

- Define the principle or rule and show how concepts and ideas 'hang' together to form the principle or rule.
- Get the trainee to express the principle or rule in his or her own words.
- Present examples of the principle or rule and illustrate it by applying it to specific cases or problems.
- Let the trainee generate his or her own illustrations of the principle or rule.
- Get the trainee to apply the principle or rule to particular examples of increasing complexity, if that is appropriate.

Memory and Procedural Skills

Committing to memory all the facts, etc, needed to perform a procedural task satisfactorily may, in some cases, be quite a tall order. There are a number of devices or methods that can assist the trainee to lighten the memory load:

- *Mnemonics* are widely used as aids to remember procedures or specific information and often form the basis of check-lists. The initial letter of each activity or element of knowledge is used to form a familiar word or phrase which acts as a memory jogger by providing an association of ideas. It is useful to let trainees make up their own mnemonics to reinforce the learning. For example, INTRO could be used to remind us of the essential components of an introduction to a training session –

Interest   **N**eed   **T**itle   **R**evision   **O**bjectives

Similarly, we might remember a code or form number because it is made up of birth dates and someone's initials.

The following example was made up by a trainee to help her to remember a seven point plan for selection interviewing:

Pam	–	**P**hysical
And	–	**A**ttainment
Gerry	–	**G**eneral intelligence
Swing	–	**S**pecial aptitudes
In	–	**I**nterests
Disco	–	**D**isposition
Clubs	–	**C**ircumstances

● *Anecdotes* serve not only to assist the memory but they make explanations more interesting. The personal story or the cautionary tale of what went wrong when a stage in a procedure was missed out is not easily forgotten. Taking the anecdote a stage further we can develop stories or verbal illustrations which will come to mind when the trainee is faced with a real situation. The following illustration was given during the training of customer service staff in a departmental store:

> Let's imagine that we have an angry customer waving a dress in front of us which she says she bought last week and when she went to put it on last night to go to a function she found that it was torn. We might react defensively by immediately offering a refund or we might disbelieve her and challenge her claims. I have encountered the most unlikely true stories which include those customers who have had garments for over a year, those who have damaged garments themselves and even those who have taken items off the peg and pretend that they are returning them because they are the wrong size. That is why, to protect the company and the genuine customer, we go through this procedure ...

● *Visual aids and job aids* are often neglected during one-to-one training. It has been mentioned already that the writing pad serves the same purpose as a flip chart. One of the benefits of writing something neatly on a pad is that the trainee can keep the sheets afterwards. Other visual aids that are of use in explaining procedures are the 'family trees' and procedural charts which were described in Chapter 3. These form the basis of job guides which help the trainee until they no longer need the prop of a reminder. When devising a job guide, it is important to ensure that it is not at variance with operational practice. The ring binder propped up on a desk with well-prepared visual aids inside plastic wallets provides an ideal equivalent of the flip chart or a substitute for an overhead projector. In fact, photocopies of the 'originals' or artwork for overhead projector transparencies enhance the professionalism of the trainer.

Teaching Form-filling

Amongst the most frequently taught subject matter related to procedural tasks is how to fill in forms. Some organizations have hundreds if not thousands of forms or their screen-based equivalents being used in their many departments. Unfortunately, even though accurate form-filling is an important part of people's tasks, it can be a painful and tedious process to be taught, and to teach, how to fill them in. Some trainers find the subject so uninspiring that they convince themselves that if the trainee is told which form to use, they ought to be able to fill it in correctly.

Problems arise when errors and omissions occur as a result of the inadequately trained job holder not knowing why certain parts of the form need to be filled in. A study of clerical staff working in a financial environment showed that the most common errors were errors of omission. Trainers will find it more interesting for themselves and the trainee if they concentrate on the reason why things are done. Even forms begin to come to life when it is known why information is asked for and particularly when the trainee is involved in trying to work out why. Such questions as:

- Why do you think we need the person's date of birth?
- What do you think the purpose is of having different coloured forms?
- Why do we need to know what their salary is?
- Why does the signature need to be witnessed?
- How do you think the manager will use this piece of information?
- Why do you think that we send the third copy to the marketing department?

keep both trainer and trainee involved as information about conventions, special instructions, legal requirements, etc, are shared. There is also scope for examples and cautionary tales to illustrate the consequences of error and omission.

The trainer will find it useful to have a number of specimen forms which contain different information from which learning points can be made.

Explanation and Demonstration of Interpersonal Skills

As mentioned in Chapter 3, considerable emphasis is placed on interpersonal skills in service industries or jobs that involve contact with clients and customers. Individuals very often acquire these skills on-the-job through interaction or working with colleagues or superiors, who may act in the role of one-to-one trainers. In order to organize and carry out an effective one-to-one training session or programme in interpersonal skills the trainer needs to consider the following issues:

● *Identifying key or critical behaviours.* Only by identifying clusters of key or critical behaviours relevant to successful social interaction in particular situations can the trainer develop the relevant objectives and learning points. These can be determined either by observing individuals who are regarded as successful in using interpersonal skills or by talking to them and getting them to pinpoint the critical and non-verbal behaviours. Verbal behaviour may include style of questioning, level of vocabulary, etc, and non-verbal behaviour would cover posture, gesture, tone of voice, pace, etc.

● *Demonstration or modelling.* A great deal of interpersonal skills learning comes about from observing others. In the training context the clusters of key or critical behaviours must be presented or demonstrated to the trainee in order that he or she is aware of what has to be learned. The presentation or demonstration can be done several ways:

— *'Live'*: the trainer or a good performer is observed in a natural setting displaying, performing or enacting the relevant behaviours.
— *'Live' role play*: A script or loose scenario is played out by the trainer and another individual or by a skilled performer and a well-briefed 'actor'.
— *'Live' video*: In some circumstances it may be possible to video a 'live' performance and then present it to the trainee.

  – *Video scripted role play*: These may be bought 'off the shelf' from commercial companies or tailor-made for particular training situations.

Whichever means is used to present or demonstrate the key behaviours, it is vital that:

  – the key or critical behaviours are clearly shown and observable;
  – the trainee must see the person who displays the key or critical behaviours as credible and must be able to identify with him or her;
  – the key or critical behaviours must be presented, where appropriate, in graduated steps moving from simple to complex and easy to difficult-to-handle situations;
  – irrelevant or distracting material must be excluded from the demonstration.

Given these requirements it is easier to pick out the advantages and disadvantages of the different methods of presenting examples of the application of interpersonal skills.

Naturally, prior to observing the demonstration, the trainee would need to be given a thorough briefing as to the purpose of the demonstration and the specific key or critical behaviours under examination.

• *Practice and Rehearsal.* The acquisition of interpersonal skills is unlikely to be achieved simply by observing a skilled practitioner or model. Practice and rehearsal are usually essential features of any one-to-one social skills training programme. There are at least four sets of activity that might be included in such a programme – micro-skills exercises, role play, 'live' enactment and reflection and mental rehearsal.

Micro-skills exercises

Before practising a particular set of interpersonal skills it is often found useful to undertake short exercises that concentrate on specific skills or sub-sets of the overall skill. For example, in training people in counselling skills, separate exercises focusing on questioning, listening or non-verbal behaviour could be introduced. The trainer might, for instance, get the trainee to practise the 'funnel' questioning technique (ie, open questions followed by probing or closed questions) by getting him or her to carry out a short interview with the trainer or a well-briefed 'actor' on a topic such as feelings about job changes or career moves.

METHOD OF DEMONSTRATION	ADVANTAGES	DISADVANTAGES
'Live'	– Dealing with a real situation makes the model's behaviour more credible.	– Unpredictable and uncontrolled. Learning points and key behaviours may not be displayed in a distinctive manner.
	– Trainees can quiz the model about why he or she performed in a particular way.	– Unexpected events or developments may occur and act as a distraction.
	– Trainees can get experience in giving feedback which may enhance their retention or the key or critical behaviours.	– Presence of a third party, ie, trainee and trainer may be inhibiting.
'Live' role play	– Trainer has a greater degree of control over the demonstration.	– Artificial and contrived; not spontaneous.
	– The demonstration can be repeated.	– Cost of preparing scripts and role players.
'Live' video	– Advantages of 'live' performance plus review facilities which allows key or critical behaviours to be seen again and discussed.	– Certain lack of control over the nature and development of the interaction between the model and the customer or client.
		– The model may feel inhibited and constrained knowing the performance is being video-taped. (*Note:* taping the performance without the permission or prior knowledge of the model is questionable ethically).
Video scripted role play	– Advantages of 'live' role play plus video review facilities.	– Disadvantages of 'live' role play.

Role play

The trainee might practise all of the relevant interpersonal skills by means of role playing. The trainer or a fully-briefed 'actor' plays the role of interviewee, client or customer. The trainee could be given the opportunity to experiment with alternative ways of using key or critical behaviours, particularly if the trainer employs the episodic approach (Brinstead, 1986). In this approach the role play is stopped at significant points, usually after a few minutes, so that the trainer and trainee can consider what took place. As a result the trainee might be directed to repeat the episode using a different tactic or to move on to the next phase of the interaction. The trainee could take part in a series of role playing scenarios that progress from simple to more complex situations.

The advantage of role playing in general, and the episodic approach in particular, is that the learning process is more controlled. Furthermore, employing video recording facilities to give feedback to the trainee greatly enhances this process.

'Live' enactment

No matter how good the simulation, interpersonal skills can only be learned properly by being exercised in a natural setting. Therefore, an essential part of any one-to-one interpersonal skills programme must require the trainee, at some point, to face real customers, clients, etc. There are at least two ways in which the trainer can introduce this experience into the programme. One way would be for the trainee to conduct all phases of a social interaction, ie, interview or discussion, while the trainer acts as an observer. Obviously a suitable explanation for this arrangement would have to be given to the other person involved. After the interaction has been completed the trainer can then give feedback.

An alternative arrangement would require the trainer to take the main responsibility for the interaction with the other party whilst the trainee 'comes in' periodically according to a pre-planned schedule. This alternative arrangement could then be followed by feedback and subsequently the trainee taking full responsibility for future interactions. As with role playing, the trainer should task the trainee with relatively straightforward situations before moving on to more complex interactions. A major drawback in adopting either of the above strategies is the fact that the trainer and trainee have less control over the learning process by comparison with episodic role playing. If 'natural' breaks could be introduced during the course of these interactions then some form of intermediate feedback could be given to the trainee, which might consequently lead to a change in strategy or tactics in subsequent phases.

Reflection and mental rehearsal

Reflection and mental rehearsal are learning activities that were referred to in Chapter 2. They are useful methods to include as part of an interpersonal skills one-to-one programme. For example, trainees could be encouraged to imagine how they might use key interpersonal skills in conducting a disciplinary interview by:

- mentally rehearsing how they will ask questions to clarify facts;
- reflecting on all of the different replies that might be offered;
- imagining how they will react to the replies that are offered;
- mentally rehearsing giving reprimands, if they are justified, etc.

Such mental rehearsal has proved to be a valuable accompaniment to the more traditional approaches described above. It is particularly valuable to introduce reflection and mental rehearsal just after trainees have observed a model and prior to role playing or 'live' enactment. (A fuller treatment of this training tactic as an approach to interpersonal skills learning can be found in Decker and Nathan, 1985).

- *Feedback and reinforcement.* In Chapter 2 the importance of feedback and reinforcement was emphasized. Feedback provides the trainee with information about the effect or consequence of a performance or the manner in which such a performance was carried out. The learning and skilful application of key or critical interpersonal behaviours can be brought out by the trainer reinforcing such behaviours through praise and encouragement and by giving informative, descriptive feedback – that is, feedback that avoids value judgements like 'good' or 'wrong', and that uses tactfully worded criticism to discourage less appropriate forms of behaviour.

In the main, feedback and reinforcement should accompany, or be given very soon after the trainee has exercised, the key or critical behaviours. In role playing both the trainer and the 'actor' can supply the trainee with feedback. However, the trainer must manage the feedback sessions so that the principles of good feedback are not broken. With 'live' enactment the feedback should be provided at a debriefing session immediately following the social situation in which the key or critical behaviours were being used. In some circumstances the customer, client or other party might be asked to comment on how well the trainee handled the interaction. However, for this to happen the trainer would need to know the client or customer well and take careful account of any ethical considerations.

The following guidelines help to make feedback effective:

- Invite the trainee to comment on their own performance first. No one likes to be told what they already know, especially when it relates to poor performance.
- Focus on what actually happened rather than what should have happened.
- Ask questions to draw out relevant comments from the trainee about their performance. Feedback is always more effective if the trainee arrives at his or her own conclusions rather than receiving a string of statements from the trainer.
- Ensure that strengths as well as development areas are discussed. Trainees are usually quick to point out areas which they feel were weak but are more reluctant to say that they did something well.
- Ensure that feedback is relevant to the performance that has been observed and avoid comparisons with other trainees.
- Do not get involved in arguments. Concentrate on what happened and what was said. Video can often help to focus on the important issues. However, there is no reason why the trainer should not express a personal reaction to behaviour which reflected anxiety, anger, frustration, etc, for example, 'I felt a little uncomfortable when you said ...'
- Consider the value of the feedback to the trainee by being aware of their personal limitations and concentrating on areas that can be improved.
- Ensure that feedback is clear, tactful and constructive.
- Do not overload the trainee with too much information irrespective of how relevant it is.
- Encourage the trainee to identify those key areas which, if improved, could result in the greatest improvement in their performance. Comments such as 'If I were you ...' are not constructive.
- Draw up an action plan with the trainee and keep a copy so that there is a framework for discussion when the trainee is next observed.
- Always try to finish on a high note by acknowledging the things that were done well.

● *Transfer of training.* An important issue for any trainer is whether trainees are able to put into practice what they have learned in training.

103

Positive transfer will have taken place if they are able to make the transition from being in a training environment to performing the job in reality. There are two forms of positive transfer:

— *specific or pure transfer*: this is when the skill or task learned in training is performed in precisely the same way in the work environment, eg, operating a circuit printing machine.
— *generalizable transfer*: this is when the trainee learns to perform skills and tasks in training in ways which are similar, but not identical, to the ways in which they are performed in the work environment, eg, conducting an appraisal interview.

Generalizable transfer is particularly important in training in interpersonal skills. The following guidelines assist in making this form of transfer effective:

— Make the training environment as realistic as possible. This is particularly pertinent to role playing, but even with 'live' enactment it is important to ensure that the situations that the trainee is exposed to are not 'too easy' otherwise the level of transfer will be low.
— Give ample opportunity to practise and rehearse the key interpersonal skills to the point where reactions and responses come naturally or with ease.
— Introduce a variety of contexts in which to learn and practise the key interpersonal skills. In role playing this helps the trainee to apply more easily what has been learned in training to the less predictable aspects of the real job.
— Avoid sessions in which the trainee is 'drilled' in interpersonal skills. This kind of rote learning tends to discourage transfer.
— Show the value of the interpersonal skills that are learned in training to the problems or issues that occur in the work setting. A trainee's motivation to succeed in training is strongly influenced by his or her perception of its value. This in turn has a strong effect on transfer.

Consolidation

It is just as important to consolidate or conclude training as it is to introduce it properly. Many sound training sessions which have been introduced perfectly tend to fall flat or drift away at the end. Each individual session, as well as the training programme as a whole, needs

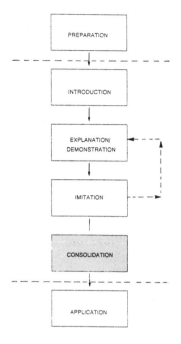

to be neatly rounded off. The point is taken that when training is continuous, sessions tend to merge throughout the day. However, if each 'chunk' is properly started and finished, both trainer and trainee feel comfortable with what they have done.

As with the introduction there is no set sequence and the headings listed below should be regarded as a menu from which those which are relevant can be selected and sequenced by the trainer.

Headings to Consolidate a Training Session

• Summary

It is quite likely that summaries will have been used at stages throughout the session. A final summary draws together everything that has been said and done by the trainer and the trainee. During the summary it is often useful to highlight questions the trainee may have asked, difficulties that might have been encountered and to re-emphasize critical points that could result in serious consequences if not done properly.

105

- **Level of achievement**

In the introduction to each session the objectives of the training will have been clarified. Trainees need reinforcement throughout their training and they like to measure their achievement against the targets that have been set. It is important to re-state what the objectives were and to either tell the trainee whether they have achieved them, or to ask the trainee if they feel they have achieved the targets. When objectives have not been met, the trainer has a duty to point out the shortcomings in performance, to give advice and to plan the way forward. This might involve remedial work, further practice, moving on more quickly, omitting some parts of the training or, in extreme cases, discontinuing training.

- **Praise**

Just as knowledge of progress is a motivator, so is recognition of achievement. When good progress has been made or difficult tasks have been learned quickly praise should be given. However, care should be taken not to devalue the effects by constantly praising satisfactory performance.

- **Reinforce the motivational message**

At the outset the trainee was given the reason why they were learning a particular task. This related to its context in the job as a whole and may have stressed its value, importance or the consequences of error, particularly if the task tended to be repetitive or boring. This message is worth reinforcing to develop a positive attitude to performing the task.

- **Look forward to the next session**

The next session may follow straight on although it is usually found to be better if a short break is taken even if it is only a 'comfort break' of a few minutes. Looking forward to what is going to be learned next not only keeps the sessions in context but provides a little more motivation.

- **Do not introduce new material**

New material should not be included in the consolidation of a training session. A consolidation draws together the threads of what has been done. While it is often a useful strategy to 'whet the appetite' for what may be coming later in the training, there is a danger in focusing the trainee's attention away from the session that has just been taught.

● **Do not ask questions to test understanding**

There is no strict dividing line between the stages of the one-to-one training model or what should be contained in each section. The practised trainer's delivery should flow from one stage to the next without it being noticeable. However, if the aim of consolidation is to tie up loose ends and draw to a satisfactory conclusion it would be better to ask and to answer questions during the demonstration – explanation – imitation stages. The flow and structure of the session can become ragged if the trainer has to back-track to confirm learning or to answer questions on subject matter that the trainee may not understand.

It was stated earlier that the headings for the consolidation stage should be regarded as a menu from which the trainer can choose and arrange in an order which suits her or his own style and which is appropriate to the session which has been taught. The example given below shows how this might be done.

Example

> Well done! You picked that up very quickly. You will remember that we set out to learn how to deal with over-payments and under-payments so that you would be able to complete the right pre-formatted letters and annotate the customer's account. We actually managed to find two or three real examples in today's work and after some practice on the specimens that I had prepared, you dealt with those for the real customer accounts. You had no problem with selecting and completing the letters but you had difficulty in calling up the customer's account on the computer. Remember that you key in only the initial letter and the first four figures of the invoice number.
>
> We'll have a short break now and then we'll go on to see how we deal with non-payment of accounts.

Headings to Consolidate the Training Programme

The consolidation of the training programme could also be the debriefing if the trainer is the trainee's supervisor or line manager. Otherwise, the consolidation prepares the trainee for the debriefing. The headings are very much the same as for the end of a training session but are wider in their scope.

● **Review of training content**

Training may have taken place over a matter of days or even weeks and sometimes it is difficult for the trainee to remember all of the ground

107

that has been covered. When the trainer has maintained a check-list of topics to be covered and has 'signed off' each topic, the trainee has been able to monitor his or her own progress. If this has not been done, the trainer needs to remind the trainee of the ground covered by reviewing what has been done in support of each of the training objectives.

• Level of competence

At the end of the training programme the trainee should have reached a level of competence which is sufficient to allow him or her to perform a job to a standard which has been specified as the target for the end of training. Trainees should be told precisely where they stand with regard to that target and, when it is necessary, the trainer should explain why further training or close supervision will be recommended. When the trainee has done well it should be confirmed that their progress and attainment will be fed back to the sponsors of their training.

• Action plan

It may be necessary or useful for the trainee to undertake some additional study or practice either to consolidate what has been learned or for developmental reasons if the trainee shows signs of being a high-flyer. Such action plans should be shared with the sponsor during the debrief.

• Trainer performance

Everything that has been discussed so far relates to the performance of the trainee. However, the whole learning process should be a partnership between the trainer and the trainee and if feedback has not been asked for on a session-by-session basis, it should be asked for now. The trainee should be asked to consider and explain how the trainer helped or hindered their training. Areas that might be considered are clarifying objectives, allowing sufficient practice, clarity of explanations, speed, etc. If it is considered that this might cause embarrassment for the trainee, a simple questionnaire can be used.

Application

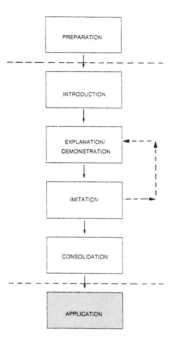

Application is the final stage in the model. It could be thought that once the training has been completed the trainer's task is complete. However, when the trainer has to work with or supervise the former trainee, the task is not complete. When the trainer is not closely involved on a day-to-day basis with the former trainee, it is still important to accept a level of accountability. The standards that are normally set for training are those which meet the minimum acceptable level of performance to undertake the job. In many cases this standard is exceeded by a considerable margin but in most cases the former trainee is likely to have to build on knowledge, speed, accuracy and confidence in order to reach the standard of an experienced worker.

When the trainer is not the line manager or supervisor, it is of value, whenever possible, to find out how well an individual is performing after training. Not only does this give the trainer a feeling of satisfaction when their 'prodigy' performs well, but it provides an opportunity to obtain feedback on areas where the training might have been better.

When the trainer is the line manager or supervisor, areas for further development of the former trainee can be identified and taken forward by planned on-the-job coaching.

5 Coaching

▷   SUMMARY   ◁

In this chapter you will learn about:
- The purposes of coaching.
- The structure of coaching programmes.
- The skills of coaching.

It was stated at the beginning of this book that organizations achieve their objectives by people doing their jobs properly and in order to do this they need to be trained. However, training is not a once and for all activity, it is a continuous process throughout our working lives. Managers and supervisors are responsible for 'achieving results' through other people. They are tasked with making the most effective use of current manpower resources and, often, with preparing individual subordinates for the future. In this latter respect they may be an integral part of an organization's succession planning and development strategy. As a great deal of learning takes place through on-the-job experiences, managers and supervisors must look to identifying or creating opportunities within this context to enhance performance improvement and development. In addition to one-to-one training, on-the-job coaching can be a major contributor to these processes.

Coaching was defined in Chapter 2 as '...developing the ability and experience of trainees by giving them systematically planned and progressively more "stretching" tasks to perform coupled with continuous appraisal and counselling'. This suggests the individual has acquired certain basic competencies or skills and that coaching is a process by which further improvement can be made through discussion and guided activity.

Pareek and Venkataswara (1990) have identified some of the main reasons for undertaking the coaching of subordinates:

- To enable the subordinate to better appreciate his or her strengths and weaknesses.
- To encourage the subordinate to establish goals or targets for further performance improvement.
- To monitor and review the subordinate's progress in achieving goals or targets.
- To identify any problems that might be adversely affecting progress.
- To assist the subordinate in generating alternatives and an action plan for dealing with problems that have been identified.
- To improve the subordinate's understanding of the work environment.
- To assist the subordinate to realize his or her potential.

In the broader sense Megginson and Boydell (1979) suggest that coaching enables the trainee to mature and makes them more capable learners. This 'moves' them in a number of ways:

● **From dependence to independence**. With improved capability the trainee acquires greater confidence leading to a greater sense of control and autonomy. This in turn means that the trainees are likely to acquire 'learning to learn' skills and become more active learners who are prepared to take a greater responsibility for their learning and be open to novel experiences that make them more flexible in their approach to new challenges.

● **From ignorance to understanding**. The development of skills through coaching should give the trainee a greater insight and understanding into both his or her immediate work environment and also into how the job fits into the wider organizational context. This can have a very positive effect on the individual's job satisfaction and motivation.

● **From superficial to in-depth employment of skills**. Coaching should broaden and deepen the trainee's use of skills and abilities. Tackling more complex problems and new experiences extends the trainee's capabilities and probably prevents job dissatisfaction stemming from their narrow and shallow application.

● **From predictability to an acceptance of ambiguity and risk**. By extending the trainee's knowledge and skills, coaching enables him or her to move away from the need for predictability towards tolerating greater ambiguity and risk in the tasks, assignments, etc. he or she undertakes.

In order to achieve the objectives of coaching and to help the trainee to develop broadly in the direction described above, the coach needs to structure the session appropriately, to exercise a repertoire of interpersonal skills and to adopt attitudes and a style which will give the best return for their efforts.

Structure of Coaching

The main features which make up well-structured coaching are as follows.

Identify or Create the Opportunity

Coaching is about extending and developing an individual's knowledge and skill. Megginson and Boydell (1979) maintain that two different sets of activities or opportunities in the work situation would allow this to happen; ongoing work routine and special assignments and job changes. In the former there are usually aspects of relative weakness that arise in 'key result areas' and coaching is the obvious means by which improvement can be brought about.

Opportunities under the second heading, special assignments, could include:

- Preparation for promotion.
- Planned delegation.
- Covering holidays and sickness, etc.
- Numerous development projects on service, procedures or products.
- Secondments to special working parties.

Managers and supervisors should be alert at all times to possibilities arising from either of these sets of activities if they are going to fulfill their role outlined at the beginning of this chapter.

Establish the Right Atmosphere and Adopt a Helpful Attitude

This is an ongoing requirement for all effective managers and supervisors. They should set high standards, set a good example and

113

communicate the benefits of, and support for, personal development and improvement. They should not cause anxiety or fear regarding the consequences of making mistakes. Rather, they should clearly show that although mistakes must be avoided where possible, nevertheless, if mistakes do occur then putting them right should be seen as a learning opportunity.

Exercise Appropriate Coaching Skills and Attitudes

These will be discussed in depth in the next section. Suffice it to say at this point that appropriate coaching skills and attitudes are complementary; you cannot really have one without the other. Essentially they are not compensatory; you cannot fully make up for a lack of skills by supportive and encouraging attitudes or vice-versa.

Set Objectives for Learning and Improvement

In many instances the trainee is being coached in order to improve some aspect of his or her performance. Simply exhorting him or her to 'do your best' to bring about improvement may have a very limited motivational impact. It is better if the trainee is working toward a clearly defined objective that is time-bounded, measurable, achievable, stretching and timely. Preferably, the manager or supervisor and the trainee should not only have decided jointly on the area or areas for improvement but also on the objectives to be achieved. Such participation is more in line with the philosophy of coaching being advocated in this chapter.

In addition to objectives for task improvement, the trainee and coach should also agree what learning objectives should be achieved. This may be particularly relevant for coaching opportunities coming under the special assignments label. The learning objectives that are set may be related to new knowledge, skills, attitudes or personal development.

Agree an Action Plan

Here again, it is important that the coach and trainee discuss and jointly agree any action plan, having, of course, first established the coaching opportunity to be pursued. The action plan, which need not be written down, should clearly indicate who will be responsible for doing what and what help or assistance would be available.

Review Progress and Provide Assistance

It is extremely important that the coach and trainee periodically review progress toward the task or learning objectives. The coach will need to exercise relevant interpersonal skills and adopt a supportive attitude in order to encourage the trainee to be forthcoming about any problems or difficulties he or she may face.

In many circumstances, the coach may have to provide direct assistance to the trainee or refer him or her to someone who can, in order to help the trainee to overcome the difficulty. Ideally, for the sake of the trainee's development, the coach should try to guide the trainee, through questioning, to solve his or her own problem or difficulty.

Review and Confirm New Learning

Whether or not the task objectives have been achieved should not minimize the importance of reviewing the learning objectives. Of particular significance are the implications of what has been achieved in respect of how the trainee tackles similar or related situations in the future. Of course, it is critical that the trainee is given further opportunities to reinforce and consolidate the new learning. Letting new knowledge and skills lie fallow is a recipe for frustration and job dissatisfaction.

Skills of Coaching

The skills of coaching are those which are actually employed in the coaching sessions. They include the following:

Physically Attending and Listening

The coach must pay close attention to and listen to the trainee throughout the coaching session. Above all, the coach must ensure that trainees are aware that full attention is being given to them. This can be done verbally and non-verbally. The kind of questions posed and the suggestions made by the coach are just two ways of indicating an attentive attitude by verbal means and these will be looked at a little later on. Positive and helpful non-verbal attending behaviours include relaxed posture, periodic eye contact, leaning slightly forward towards the trainee, etc. Naturally, staring, interrupting, unfriendly looks, etc, might demonstrate an attentive attitude but they are hardly likely to create a positive climate for the coaching discussion.

Strange as it may seem, remaining silent may indicate good attention, particularly if it is accompanied by some non-verbal attentive behaviour such as nodding. Often the converse, ie, being too quick to fill the silence by asking questions or by replying to a question, can be seen as a poor demonstration of attending.

Active listening can also be shown through the techniques of paraphrasing and reflecting on what has just been said. *Paraphrasing* involves the listener repeating back, not verbatim but in his or her own words, what he or she thinks the speaker has just said. This is a way of 'checking out' the content of what the speaker has communicated. Of course, it goes without saying that the listener should paraphrase at appropriate points in the discussion, eg, after critical contributions by the speaker, rather than on a haphazard or random basis.

Whereas paraphrasing focuses on the content of the speaker's message, *reflection* is more concerned with feelings and emotions. The coach 'listens' to how the other person feels or what has remained unsaid and then feeds it back to him or her in a sensitive or tactful manner. For example the trainee might say: 'The people in IT have put up all sorts of obstacles preventing me from going ahead. This means that the other deadlines are having to be put back'. The coach in reply, and attempting to reflect the trainee's feelings, might respond: 'You feel frustrated by the reaction of IT and this is making you a little anxious about the other targets you're required to reach'. The good coach does not avoid talking about a trainee's emotions, as these may be acting as blockages to his or her learning and development, hence the importance for the coach of acquiring the skill and confidence to use reflection.

Asking Questions

The coach needs to be skilful in employing questioning techniques in order to get the trainee to talk about his or her feelings, problems or ideas. The kinds of question that help the coach to explore these issues constructively are:

- **Open questions.** These sorts of question are relatively short and usually begin with words such as 'What...', 'When...', 'How...' or 'Where...'. Although the word 'Why' could also be included in this list it must be used sparingly as it could be perceived by the trainee as indicating an interrogative attitude on the part of the coach.

- **Probe questions.** These questions often follow on from the answers to open questions. The intention of such questions is to get the speaker to give clarification, or elaborate further on the original answer. As with open questions, probes can begin with words like 'How...', 'What...', etc. Sometimes probe questions seek ideas concerning a problem brought to the surface by means of an open question, eg, 'What are the alternative ways of handling that difficulty?'

● **Comparative questions**. 'How does that compare with this?', 'In what ways does that differ from this?' are examples of comparative questions. They may function as open or probe questions.

Questions the coach should try to avoid in coaching sessions are:

● **Leading questions**. The coach might inadvertently ask a question that supplies the sort of answer he or she was looking for. This may not reflect the real answer that the trainee wished to give as either he or she might not want to contradict the coach or is simply happy to go along with what the coach is suggesting, eg, 'So that phase had to be aborted because they failed to meet their obligations?'

● **Critical questions**. A coaching session should be a constructive and positive experience for the trainee, raising and not destroying his or her confidence. This is very unlikely to be the case if the questions posed by the coach are critical or raise obvious doubts about the trainee's competence. Such questions on their own or accompanied by sarcasm will, no doubt, lead to a negative attitude towards the coaching process. Furthermore, testing questions, which can be usefully employed in one-to-one training, might be viewed by the trainee in a coaching session as indicating a critical or superior attitude on the part of the coach.

● **Closed questions**. Although, on occasions, the coach may wish to seek specific information through closed questions of the 'Did you ...' variety, a discussion dominated by these sorts of question may turn out to be rather restricted. The trainee may respond in a very limited way which is contrary to the spirit of effective coaching. The conversational balance becomes too coach-orientated rather than trainee-centred.

Generating Options and Making Suggestions

Where it is possible, the coach should attempt to encourage the trainee to come up with ideas and suggestions for improvement or development which they can then both evaluate. However, there may be occasions when the coach is the obvious source of feasible options or alternatives. He or she should put them forward as suggestions for consideration by the trainee only after the trainee has exhausted his or her approaches first, and not as definitive proposals. Even if an idea has not come from the trainee he or she can still feel a sense of ownership and commitment towards it provided that the evaluation process is a joint effort. Above all, the coach must avoid creating dependency in the trainee, which can easily come about if the coach always takes the lead in suggesting ideas, options or alternatives.

Giving Feedback

Some of the principles of giving feedback in a constructive manner have already been discussed in previous chapters. In coaching situations it makes good sense for the coach and the trainee to discuss at the outset the purpose and value of feedback. This may help to prevent defensive and negative reactions on the part of the trainee. Such reactions include:

- Laughing off feedback that suggests a need for improvement.
- Being aggressive towards the coach instead of getting him or her to explain the feedback.
- Making excuses instead of considering and trying to understand why performance failed to reach required standards.
- Passively accepting feedback without exploring further with the coach its nature and the implications.
- Displaying doubts, even cynicism, about whether improvement can be achieved rather than planning to bring it about in the future.

Feedback, to be effective, should consolidate and confirm the new knowledge and skills learned and attitudes adopted by the trainee and reinforce what the trainee has performed well.

Attitudes and Behaviours that Support the Coaching Process

Apart from the skills outlined above, there are a number of attitudes and behaviours which need to be shown at various stages if the full aims and objectives of coaching are to be achieved. Some of these have already been highlighted; other critical positive attitudes and behaviours are:

- Showing genuine concern for the trainee or subordinate in order to establish an effective and helpful relationship.
- Influencing the trainee towards developing greater autonomy and making his or her own decisions.
- Positively reinforcing a trainee's success so as to encourage him or her to be more pro-active and to take more initiatives.
- Encouraging the trainee to think through issues and to come up with ideas.

- Demonstrating clearly that the development of subordinates is viewed as important.
- Adopting a participative management style that involves the trainee in all key stages.
- Giving due attention to the trainee's weaknesses and exploring together ways that they can be overcome.
- Allowing the trainee to explore and expand the boundaries and limits of his or her abilities by presenting new challenges and experiences and by setting objectives which stretch ability.
- Emphasizing the importance of teamwork and mutual support between coach and trainee.

Attitudes and Behaviours that Undermine the Coaching Process

In addition to the opposites of the positive attitudes and behaviours set out above, the coach may also express other views, opinions and beliefs and act in ways that may have a negative impact on the coaching relationship. Some of the more damaging of these negative attitudes and behaviours are:

- Being too supervisory and directive, ie, telling rather than listening, and leaving too little room for the trainee to show initiative.
- Creating dependency by either imposing solutions on the trainee or being too quick to suggest ideas or ways forward.
- In giving feedback, placing too much emphasis on the trainee's failures or weaknesses.
- Supporting a 'divide and rule' policy amongst subordinates or trainees.
- Being too judgemental and not listening to the trainee's views with an open mind and with respect.
- Trying to be too clever and to win or score a point against the trainee.
- Attempting to solve the trainee's problems.
- Becoming involved in, or provoking, an argument with the trainee, thus creating a defensive and restrictive climate.
- Not remaining objective and becoming too embroiled or personally involved in the situation or problem.

Many of these negative behaviours come about when the coach feels threatened by the expertise which is being developed by the trainee. In many ways the barriers which prevent managers from delegating are relevant in a coaching role. Perhaps the most threatening of these is the subconscious or even conscious thought that by teaching subordinates too much, one's own position and value can be eroded.

As organizations review and revise their concepts of a trained workforce and of the hierarchical shape of an organization, so teamwork, flexible use of staff and planned succession take a higher profile. Those who are involved in coaching cannot be expected to adapt easily and readily to a role which could be alien or threatening to them. Investment in the selection and training of those involved in one-to-one training and in coaching is a vital link in training policy if any real value is to be gained from the use of these methods of developing the workforce.

6

Selection, Training and Development of One-to-one Trainers and Coaches

> ### SUMMARY ◁

In this chapter you will learn about:
- The knowledge, skills, attitudes and qualities required of a good one-to-one trainer and coach.
- The training and development of one-to-one trainers and coaches.
- How to get feedback from students.

Most of us become involved in training others at some stage during our working lives. For many, it is seen as 'showing' someone how to do something and it is not realized that this means 'training' or that they are, in fact, trainers. In Chapter 1 it was shown that in Great Britain in 1986–7, 60.7 million days were spent on on-the-job training. No doubt, that figure would have been considerably higher had it been possible to count all of the training days that had not been recognized as such.

There are a number of ways in which people become responsible for training and development on a one-to-one basis.

- By force of circumstances when no one else is available and someone needs to be trained. Whoever happens to be available at the time is given the task.

- By delegation when training is seen as a developmental activity for someone and they are given the opportunity to exercise this responsibility. Sometimes, this form of delegation is aimed at testing to see whether someone is capable of training others.
- By virtue of the expertise that someone has. Those who are the best at performing a task are often selected to train others in the belief that there could be no one better than a technical 'expert'.
- By nature of the job when training is included in someone's job description.
- By choice, when someone enjoys helping others to learn and in order to gain additional job satisfaction, they seek opportunities to become involved in training.

However, even those who undertake training willingly or with the best of motives, may not necessarily be the best people for the job, especially if they have not been trained. The way in which people become involved in one-to-one training or coaching does not predict how well or how badly they will perform. Good and bad practice has been seen in both those who want to be trainers and those who have been tasked.

The most commonly observed poor qualities which reflect bad practice include:

- Adopting a highly directive style of teaching which does not allow the trainee to participate and does not confirm that learning has taken place.
- Making unrealistic assumptions about the trainee's level of knowledge or failing to establish their level of knowledge in the first place.
- Showing impatience or intolerance when trainees fail to understand or are slow to learn.
- Lacking commitment to the subject being taught or not taking the role of trainer seriously.
- Lacking in verbal/oral skills.
- Trying to teach too much too quickly.
- Refusing to accept criticism or advice on training methods.

In addition to those listed above the following negative qualities have been observed in those who coach badly:

- Failing to plan a programme so that development becomes haphazard.
- Giving non-developmental tasks that the 'coach' does not want to do.
- Interfering or taking over if the job is not being done as it should be.

— Failing to be available as a reference point or to give guidance.
— Regarding developmental training as being thrown in 'at the deep end'.
— Failing to give feedback apart from criticism when performance is lacking in some way.

No doubt readers will be able to add to the list other negative qualities which they have observed for themselves. Similarly, the list of good qualities which follows is not intended to be exhaustive but to illustrate the most frequently observed examples of good practice. Apart from the opposites to those listed above, one might add:

— Demonstrating technical competence in the area being taught.
— Showing a 'natural' ability to train and a satisfaction from and enthusiasm for doing it.
— Demonstrating a high level of interpersonal skills.
— Being a good listener and questioner.
— Showing a genuine interest in people's learning and development.

Selecting Trainers

The point was made earlier that all of us are likely to be involved in training someone else at some stage in our working lives. It might seem unnecessary, therefore, to think about the selection of one-to-one trainers or coaches. However, in many organizations there are those for whom one-to-one training takes up a large proportion of their time or who become recognized as the department's or unit's trainer in the same way that people take responsibility for First Aid when it is needed. Similarly there are some departments or units the nature of whose work lends itself to developmental opportunities and whose managers become closely involved with coaching. Close consideration should be given to the selection of those who fall into these categories.

Perhaps the greatest mistake in selecting someone to be a trainer in this context is the over-emphasis on technical ability. This is not to say that technical ability is not important; it is vital not only to ensure that correct training is given but also to establish the credibility of the trainer in the eyes of the trainee. However, it is often more appropriate to select and easier to train someone with a high level of interpersonal skills and to build up their technical expertise than to have a technical 'expert' who is seriously lacking in interpersonal skills or motivation. Parallels can be drawn with the selection of some supervisors. They are

123

selected because they are technically sound but with little attention being paid to their people skills and less to their need to be trained in the skills of front line management.

The qualities discussed earlier take us part of the way towards providing a check-list of criteria for the selection and training of one-to-one trainers and coaches. Without going into a sophisticated and costly selection procedure to identify these qualities and hence potential as a trainer, a useful profile of an individual can be built up from informal observations as well as the more formal assessment procedures that are likely to be in place already. These might include the following:

- Outside interests, particularly those which are people-oriented and which exercise interpersonal skills or which may involve teaching others, eg, coaching sports teams, chairing club and society meetings, etc.
- Informal judgements based on work relationships.
- Impressions of verbal ability.
- Simulated exercises relating to one-to-one situations.
- Formal assessments based on performance appraisal, group meetings and developmental training.

This goes part of the way to ensure that the right people are used in training. However, to get closer to being more professional in selecting trainers and subsequently in training them, one really needs a job specification for the one-to-one trainer and for those involved in coaching. Enquiries have shown that very few of these exist. In fact, it is quite understandable that training or coaching is only listed as one of a number of duties on many job descriptions that have been seen, especially when it is an infrequent activity. Nevertheless, even the 'occasional trainer' has a very important role to play when he or she undertakes that role. On some of the job specifications that have been looked at, the requirement for training and coaching listed under 'Knowledge' and 'Skills' has indicated a strong preference for technical knowledge and technical skill with little mention of the skills of the trainer.

It is not the intention here to be prescriptive about job specifications for all of those who are involved in one-to-one training and coaching. However, some aspects of the roles are presented in the format of a job specification (Figures 6.1 and 6.2) in order to give some idea of the demands made on trainers which might be considered when drawing up selection criteria and training programmes for trainers. Figure 6.1 presents aspects related to one-to-one training, and Figure 6.2 contains additional items relevant to coaching.

TASK ELEMENT	KNOWLEDGE	SKILLS	ATTITUDES
Assess training needs of individuals	• How training needs can be identified • Systematic approach to training	• Basic performance analysis • Task/skill analysis • Questioning techniques	• Appreciate costs of too little/too much training • Value the need to be systematic
Plan a programme of training	• Conditions and principles of learning • How and why people learn • Structure of training objectives • 'Hygiene factors' that contribute to an effective programme	• Task/skill analysis • Writing objectives • Sequencing/ structuring (in terms of learning conditions and timing) • Identifying appropriate learning tactics	
Prepare one-to-one training sessions	• Structure of a one-to-one training session • How individual differences affect learning • Tactics to help memory and learning • Testing/assessment techniques	• Writing session notes • Preparation of visual aids, test pieces, examples • Integrating and synchronizing tactics and learning material	• Value the need for thorough preparation
Conduct a one-to-one training session	• How individual differences affect learning • Tactics to assist learning	• Explaining • Demonstrating • Listening/observing • Questioning • Giving feedback • Counselling • Encouraging • Exercising patience	• Appreciate that people learn at different speeds and in different ways
Assess effectiveness of training	• Instruments for collecting data • Validation techniques and concepts and principles • Presentation of statistical data	• Design, plan and apply techniques for collecting data • Interpreting data	• Value need for validation of training

Figure 6.1 *Example of a job specification: One-to-one training*

TASK ELEMENT	KNOWLEDGE	SKILLS	ATTITUDES
Assess and agree developmental needs of individuals	● How developmental needs can be identified	● Interviewing ● Counselling ● Assessing potential	● Value need for succession planning and pro-active training
Assess organizational human resource needs	● How organizational structure and corporate and departmental objectives are determined		
Plan a programme of development	● Principles of delegation ● Time management ● Action plans	● Selecting developmental activities ● Negotiating	
Conduct developmental activities	● Principles of supervision ● Principles of counselling	● Identifying developmental opportunities ● Briefing ● Supervising ● Assessing/evaluating ● Counselling	● Appreciate need for individual to experience success
Assess effectiveness of developmental training	● Structure of debriefing session	● Debriefing ● Feedback ● Counselling ● Listening	● Value feedback from individual on own performance

Figure 6.2 *Example of a job specification: Coaching*

Obviously, job specifications will vary considerably depending on whether the trainer is an occasional trainer or a full-time trainer with the backing of a training section. However, the main concern is that the job holder's role as a trainer should be defined more specifically than a brief mention at the end of a list of duties. It would be expecting too much to find someone readily available with all of the knowledge and skills listed in the broad example given in Figures 6.1 and 6.2. Therefore, the selection criteria are more likely to be indicators of potential which would need to be developed by trainer training. The criteria which tend to be the most indicative are: high level of technical knowledge (or ability to acquire it), good interpersonal skills, and a desire to be involved in the training of others.

Training the Trainers

The need to train those involved in one-to-one training and coaching becomes evident from looking at the specimen job specifications in Figures 6.1 and 6.2. The decision on how much training needs to be given depends on what kind of a return the organization is seeking from the activities of the trainer. A token investment in trainer training may yield limited results but over-training the 'occasional' trainer is likely to be wasteful if much of what they have been trained in is forgotten. Time spent on, and content of, training has to be balanced against the value of the outcome.

The key areas for training that affect the proficient delivery of one-to-one and coaching sessions have been found to be:

- Understanding how people vary in aptitude, speed of learning, motivation and style of learning.
- Practice in planning and preparation of training and development programmes based on individuals and their needs.
- Practice in teaching skills, assisting and supporting learning.
- Practice in assessing one's own performance.

In the case of the 'occasional' trainer, it may be sufficient to provide written guidelines in the form of 'dos and don'ts' or a check-list to supplement the stages in the one-to-one training model. Similar guidelines could be prepared for coaching based on the coaching model and the principles of delegation. However, the skills needed for coaching often involve one-to-one training and anyone acting as a coach would benefit from developing one-to-one techniques. This would separate out the 'need to know' from the 'nice to know'. A more thorough approach might be to design a self-study package which could include the 'nice to know' as well as the 'need to know'. A useful feature of the self-study package is that it can exercise the trainer in the planning and preparation of programmes and sessions based on case study material. However, one-to-one training and coaching involve more than 'knowing' and paper-based exercises; they are skills that have to be practised and developed. Therefore, it is important that some training is given in the form of practical sessions supported by constructive feedback. The use of video during these sessions allows greater opportunity for appraisal of performance to identify strengths and development needs.

When a high level of return is demanded of trainers, it has a grim logic that they are likely to need a higher level of training. The following list of behavioural performance statements relates to training objectives which could easily form the basis of a week's course. It can also be used as a check-list to clarify the needs of all those who are involved to a greater or lesser degree in training and development on a one-to-one basis.

TRAINING OBJECTIVES FOR ONE-TO-ONE TRAINERS

1. State the purpose of training.

Enabling objectives

- Define training, on-the-job training, off-the-job training, coaching.
- State the reasons for training in organizations.
- List the benefits of effective training in organizations.
- List the costs of too much and too little training.

Attitudinal objective

- Accept that the trainer makes a positive contribution to the organization's goals.

2. Describe factors that influence how and why people learn.

Enabling objectives

- Define motivation.
- Describe how people learn.
- State reasons why people learn.
- List the most common barriers to learning.
- List the qualities of an effective one-to-one trainer.

Attitudinal objectives

- Appreciate that trainees are different in the way that they are motivated.
- Accept that the trainer plays a major role in motivating the trainee.

3. Prepare and plan a programme of instruction.

Enabling objectives

- List the information required to prepare and plan a programme of instruction, using the headings; Who, What, Why, Where and When.
- Describe the features of a well-balanced programme of instruction.
- Describe the basic conditions and principles of learning.
- List tactics and strategies to assist learning.

Attitudinal objectives

- Value the need for thorough preparation and planning of a programme of instruction.

4. Prepare and plan a one-to-one training session.

Enabling objectives

- State and describe the stages that make up a one-to-one training session.
- State the importance of having objectives.
- Write an objective for a session.
- Organize learning material into a logical order.
- State the purpose of tests and exercises.
- Compose test and exercise questions.
- Write session notes.
- Prepare visual aids, examples, etc.
- List features of a good explanation and a good demonstration.

Attitudinal objectives

- Value the need for thorough preparation and planning of a session.
- Value the need to confirm that the trainee has learned (eg, use of tests, exercises, etc).
- Value the importance of testing and questioning.

5. Teach an individual trainee.

Enabling objectives

- Apply the skills of:
  - explaining and demonstrating
  - listening and observing
  - giving feedback
  - testing and questioning
  - guiding, prompting, cueing and correcting

Attitudinal objectives

- Appreciate that the trainee regards the trainer as an expert.
- Appreciate the fact that some trainees encounter difficulty and need to be helped.
- Accept accountability for the performance of the trainee after the training has been completed.

6. Conduct a review of own teaching.

Enabling objectives

- State the importance and function of a review of teaching.
- List the factors that must be considered during a review.
- Identify strengths and development needs in own teaching.
- Develop action plans for own development.

Attitudinal objectives

- Value the need to review one's performance.
- Accept the fact that all trainers can improve their performance.

Developing the Skills of Trainers

Completion of a training programme for trainers is really only the beginning of the development of their skills. It is only when they have had the opportunity to put into practice what they have learned and to judge its effectiveness that their own personalities begin to influence the way in which they train others. It is during the first few sessions after their own training that trainers are able to discover what works for them and what doesn't, what their strengths are and what areas they need to work on. This means that they need feedback. This can be done by experienced trainers 'sitting in' and then discussing the session, by other novice trainers observing and acting as a sounding board for ideas, by discussing the session with the trainee or by answering honestly the questions on the check-list in Figure 6.3.

How well did I prepare?
How did I motivate the trainee?
How did I put the job into context?
Did I state the objective?
How did I explain the structure of the session?
Did I check the trainee's previous experience?
Was the training put over in a logical sequence and broken down into digestible chunks?
Was the session interesting?
How did I get the trainee to participate?
How did I examine the trainee's progress?
Did I identify any development areas?
Did I use effective questioning?
Did I highlight the important/key points?
How did I assess the trainee's overall performance?
Did I show confidence and enthusiasm?
Did I use my notes?
Was the training a success?
Did I follow up the training to evaluate my effectiveness?

Figure 6.3 *Self-appraisal check-list*

Trainers must be encouraged to adopt one, if not more, of these strategies if they hope to succeed as trainers. Most of us tend to dwell on what we feel are 'weaknesses' when we consider our performance. This is why it is useful to have an observer who is more effective in noting what happened during the training session. In this way strengths can be identified as well as development needs; the term 'development needs' is preferable to 'weaknesses'. The check-list in Figure 6.3 can be used as the basis of discussion between trainer and observer but essentially it is a self-appraisal check-list.

Almost invariably one-to-one training and coaching is done without supervision. This means that the trainer has a responsibility to assess him or herself continuously. Teaching and coaching should never become stale and inflexible; constant reviews enable the trainer to keep the training relevant and the style of delivery effective and enthusiastic. It improves the trainer's motivation which, in turn, will affect the movitation of the trainee.

Initially, it is useful to make notes almost formally under each question on the check-list. As experience grows, trainers find themselves automatically appraising their performance without direct reference to a check-list. However, while the enthusiastic trainer is likely to be highly perceptive and sometimes over-critical of his or her own performance, there is a danger that complacency can creep in. In order to avoid this, feedback on trainer performance should be sought from the trainee. When a good rapport has been established between trainer and trainee, comments on the trainer's performance can be asked for in a casual but objective way during sessions.

In the introduction to a training programme the trainer may establish some 'ground rules' by inviting the trainee to 'interrupt me if I am going too quickly or if there is anything that you don't understand'. Also, the reaction of a trainee during a session may prompt the trainer to ask such questions as:

> You look a bit puzzled, was my explanation difficult to understand?
> Did I go through that too quickly?
> Was that too much at one go?

In addition, a short questionnaire could be used at the end of the training programme to gauge the trainee's overall reaction. The information asked for in an end-of-programme questionnaire falls into two main categories. One category asks for details about the usefulness of the training content, how much of it is being applied, how frequently, and the level of confidence of the former trainee. The other category concentrates on the quality of the trainer's performance. While not neglecting the importance of the content of training, the intention here is to concentrate on the trainer. The questions shown in Figure 6.4 provide examples of what might be asked in an attempt to get the trainee's reaction to key areas of trainer performance.

Rate your trainer's contribution to your training on the scale shown below by ticking the box which most closely corresponds to your experience.

	6	5	4	3	2	1	
Structure of programme explained very clearly.							Structure of programme not explained at all.
Sessions well structured.							Little or no structure to sessions.
Content divided into manageable 'chunks'.							Too much information packed into each session.
Kept to subject at all times.							Constantly wandered off subject.
Explanations easy to understand.							Explanations very confusing.
Demonstrations easy to follow.							Demonstrations couldn't be followed.
Understanding checked regularly.							Never checked my understanding.
Answered my questions well.							Answered my questions badly.
Regularly told me how I was getting on.							Never told me how I was getting on.
Worked at the right pace.							Worked too fast or too slow.
Very enthusiastic.							Totally lacking in enthusiasm.
Very patient.							Quickly lost patience.
Supportive and encouraging.							Over-critical.

Figure 6.4 *Example of end-of-training questionnaire*

Conclusion

At the beginning of this book it was claimed that almost all of us, at some time during our working lives, are given the task of training another person. Very often this is described as 'showing' someone how to perform a particular task and because 'showing' is not acknowledged as being training, it is insufficiently resourced. This means that those who are involved in raising the performance or developing the skills of individuals may not be the right people for the job and are unlikely to have been trained as trainers.

One-to-one training and coaching should be regarded as integral parts of any organizational training programme and should not be regarded as getting training 'on the cheap'. The outcomes of these forms of training and development are equally as important as those of any other form of training. It follows that trainers working in this mode need to be selected carefully and trained to a level appropriate to their degree of involvement.

References

BRINSTEAD, D (1986) *Developments in Interpersonal Skills Training* Aldershot, Gower Publishing Company.

DECKER P J, and NATHAN B R (1985) *Behaviour Modelling Training – Principles and Applications* New York, Praeger.

HONEY, P and MUMFORD, A (1986) *Using your Learning Styles* (2nd ed), UK, Peter Honey.

MEGGINSON, D and BOYDELL, T (1979) *A Manager's Guide to Coaching*, London, British Association for Commercial and Industrial Education.

PAREEK, V and VENKATESWARA, R (1990) *Performance Coaching The 1990 Annual: Developing Human Resources*, San Diego, California, University Associates.

SLOMAN, M (1989) 'On-the-job Training, A Costly Poor Relation', *Personnel Management*, February.

STUART, R and HOLMES H, L (1982) 'Successful Trainer Styles', *Journal of European Industrial Training*, 6(4) 17 – 23.

WINFIELD, J (1988) *Learning to Teach Practical Skills* (2nd ed) London, Kogan Page.

Index